SIMPLE ACTS

The Busy Teen's Guide to
MAKING A DIFFERENCE

Natalie Silverstein, MPH

free spirit
PUBLISHING®

Library of Congress Cataloging-in-Publication Data
Names: Silverstein, Natalie, author.
Title: Simple acts : a busy teen's guide to making a difference / Natalie Silverstein, MPH.
Description: Minneapolis, MN : Free Spirit Publishing Inc., [2022] | Includes bibliographical references and index. | Audience: Ages 13+
Identifiers: LCCN 2021030532 (print) | LCCN 2021030533 (ebook) | ISBN 9781631986260 (paperback) | ISBN 9781631986277 (pdf) | ISBN 9781631986284 (epub)
Subjects: LCSH: Voluntarism—Juvenile literature. | Young volunteers in community development—Juvenile literature. | Young volunteers in social service—Juvenile literature. | Social action—Juvenile literature. | Social problems—Juvenile literature.
Classification: LCC HN49.V64 S583 2022 (print) | LCC HN49.V64 (ebook) | DDC 302/.14—dc23
LC record available at https://lccn.loc.gov/2021030532
LC ebook record available at https://lccn.loc.gov/2021030533

Edited by Ruthie Nelson Van Oosbree
Cover and interior design by Shannon Pourciau
Illustrated by Joanne Lew-Vriethoff

Printed in the United States of America

Free Spirit Publishing
An imprint of Teacher Created Materials
6325 Sandburg Road, Suite 100
Minneapolis, MN 55427-3674
(612) 338-2068
help4kids@freespirit.com
freespirit.com

FSC
www.fsc.org
MIX
Paper from
responsible sources
FSC® C005010

Free Spirit offers competitive pricing.
Contact edsales@freespirit.com for pricing information
on multiple quantity purchases.

Dedication

This book is dedicated to my three big-hearted teenagers/young adults—Emilia, Archie, and Alaina—and to a generation of young people whose kindness, resilience, and generosity of spirit inspire hope for our future.

Contents

Preface

This book was drafted over the course of three months in the spring of 2020. After the joy of publishing my first book, *Simple Acts: The Busy Family's Guide to Giving Back*, in 2019, I was delighted to be able to write a follow-up specifically for teens. I enthusiastically jumped into the project in early March. Within days, the world flipped upside down. Due to the growing concern around the spread of COVID-19 in our community, schools and offices were closed, and we were asked to stay at home. Along with millions of other Americans, and countless others around the globe, my family and I began a lengthy period of quarantine and isolation, social distancing, working from home, and remote learning.

During this time, several tragic, deadly incidents involving Black Americans and law enforcement sparked renewed outrage and amplified the national discussion of racism. Massive protests, often organized and led by teens and young adults, drove a worldwide reckoning on racial inequality. We were also in the midst of a contentious presidential election, and there was a heightened sense of urgency around voting rights and the importance of registering to vote so that everyone's voice could be heard. It was a time of tremendous upheaval, and illness, loss of life, financial hardship, frustration, and despair threatened to overwhelm us. While many yearned for a return to "normalcy" as we struggled in lockdown and quarantine, it became clear that going back to "the way things were before" was impossible. We needed to do better, to be better, and to work together to achieve those goals.

Over the course of the pandemic, my children, ages 12, 16, and 19, dealt with bewildering change as their lives were upended overnight. Like young people around the world, they were disconnected from friends, school, activities, and routine, and they suffered disappointments large and small. As a parent, I found it challenging to maintain my sense of optimism as I supported my children and allowed them to grieve their losses. I worried for their mental health. There were many weeks during this time when I lost motivation. I didn't know if I had the heart to finish writing this book or if the subject would resonate. The future seemed so uncertain.

Then, day by day, I watched my children emerge from their sadness with new resolve to make the best of their situation, to make lemonade out of abundant lemons, to continue to care deeply about others and the world around them. Their resilience lifted my spirits. I used my social media platform to amplify stories of generosity, kindness, and hope. I encouraged families to find ways to engage in "kitchen table kindness" activities at home. As a family, we went back to the basic principle of *Simple Acts*: do what you can, your own small bit of good. We baked cookies for first responders, wrote letters to isolated seniors, recorded birthday tributes for friends whose celebrations were canceled, sent pizzas to the ICU staff of a local hospital. We did what so many generous souls did during this time: we found small but meaningful ways to help. We couldn't fix the considerable and overwhelming problems in the world, but there was *something* we could do to ease the burden on others. Those small actions also made us feel better, as service always does, providing light during some very dark days. I was inspired to see how many people answered the call to service in my community and beyond. Following Mister Rogers's famous suggestion, I looked for the helpers, and I found them all around me.

I realized that my work in promoting family and youth service had become even more important. The message of this book is very clear, and it hasn't changed since I began writing it: you don't need to change the world to make a difference, and *everyone* has something to give. Simple, intentional acts of kindness and service, sprinkled throughout your busy everyday life, will create a positive ripple effect in your home, school, community, and the wider world. I can assure you from personal experience that this kindness practice will be a great source of comfort, motivation, and joy, getting you through even the most difficult times in your life. When you are good to others, that goodness is reflected back to you. My fervent hope is that this book will inspire you to share your goodness, your light, with a world that desperately needs it.

Natalie Silverstein

Introduction

The Truth About Being a "Changemaker"

"How Can I Change the World When I Have Homework and Basketball Practice Every Day?"

That's a great question. Here's the simple and truthful answer: you probably won't change the *whole* world. Realistically, you can't fix all of the world's problems as you sprint through your days at school, afternoons playing sports or working, and nights filled with homework (not to mention a little well-earned downtime). However, there are lots of simple things you can do every day to make the world a little kinder and gentler, to make life easier for another person, to improve your own community. This book was created to help you figure out what those things are, which ones spark your interest, and how to fit them into your hectic schedule. Here is what you need to get started: a curious mind, a caring heart, and a willingness to try. I hope this book will help you incorporate small but meaningful acts of service and kindness into your busy life.

If you watch the news or follow social media, you'll often see stories of young people doing amazing things to create positive change in the world. Teens are volunteering, starting nonprofit organizations, collecting donations, organizing protests and marches, launching social media campaigns, circulating petitions, and raising awareness. They're taking these actions in response to many important issues that impact their lives and society: hunger and homelessness, poverty and economic injustice, climate change, racism, sexism, LGBTQIA+ rights, common-sense gun legislation, mental health, immigration, bullying, and countless others. These young people are rightly gaining the attention and respect of the media and the public, helping their neighbors in need while influencing government leaders to move the needle on social policy. They aren't waiting around for others to fix the problems; they are jumping in, using their voices and their media savvy to amplify the conversations around these issues. This is amazing and inspiring work, and it reminds us that everyone should care and try to make a difference.

It can also be intimidating. The bar has been set pretty high, and tackling some of these issues in real life can be daunting. Just getting through the day, the week, the quarter, and the school year can be a challenge. Most teens take care of family responsibilities, work hard in school, hold down part-time jobs, and manage lots of other commitments. Sometimes it's a struggle—emotionally, mentally, physically, academically, and financially—to juggle all of this. Saving the world is a little too much to add to your overflowing plate.

I get it, and I hope I can provide some perspective on this whole subject. If it feels like the pressure to be a "changemaker" is overwhelming, let me share an idea you'll hear again, and which is at the heart of this book: creating change doesn't *have* to be grand or global. It doesn't have to take over your entire life, and it doesn't have to put the weight of the world on your shoulders. This book was written to inspire a more realistic approach to service for teenagers, a more organic way to make the world a better place: one simple act at a time.

But . . . Why?

You may be asking yourself, "Why is service so important for me right now?" Well, to keep it simple, I think it can change your life. In my work as a speaker, writer, and consultant on this topic, I witness firsthand the power of volunteering to change lives. I encourage children and teens (and the adults who care for them) to keep their eyes, hearts, and minds open so that they can find meaningful ways to help others. Service expands your worldview, introducing you to new people, problems, situations, organizations, and experiences. Connecting with others through service organically reminds us that we are all more similar than we are different. We find common ground. Every person we encounter is deserving of our kindness and respect. It's important to reserve judgment and to recognize that we have no idea what challenges another person is facing. There is no pity, no handout, no us-and-them mentality in meaningful service. While we are helping another person today, we will almost certainly need help ourselves someday. Like any skill, empathy (the ability to understand and share the feelings of another person) is something you need to practice. Volunteering, engaging in community service, and intentionally doing acts of kindness are easy ways to flex your empathy muscles, and I've witnessed the good that can come from that exercise.

RESEARCH SAYS GIVING BACK IS GOOD FOR YOU

But don't take just my word for it. If you need more reasons to try volunteering, there's plenty of scientific research to prove that giving back to others is also good for *you*. By every measure, adults who volunteer are happier, healthier, more connected, and less lonely. The benefits for teens who volunteer are even bigger. According to research conducted by sociologists Jane Allyn Piliavin and Erica Siegl at the University of Wisconsin, teen volunteers, even those who are considered "at risk" themselves, report a positive effect on their grades, self-concept, and attitude toward education. Youth volunteering also leads to reduced drug use and huge declines in school dropout rates and teen pregnancies. Other research shows that creating good service habits starts in the home with your family. In 2005, the Corporation for National and Community Service and the US Census Bureau conducted a national survey of over 3,000 teenagers (ages 12-18) that collected information on teen volunteering habits and school-based service learning. The survey found that kids from homes where at least one adult volunteers regularly are nearly three times as likely to volunteer on a consistent (weekly or monthly) basis. A 2012 study by DoSomething.org also found that the majority of kids and teens who volunteer do so because of personal motivation, not as a school requirement (meaning they're volunteering because they *want* to, not because someone is forcing them to do it). Kids like to keep things social—both online and in person—so it's not surprising that the same study found that three-quarters of American teens whose friends regularly volunteer also do so themselves. Forming good habits when you are young is also important. Kids who volunteer are more likely to continue volunteering as teens and adults. The best news of all: studies have shown that adults who volunteer remain physically active and socially connected, leading to happier, healthier, and longer lives. Please note, when I say "socially connected," I mean in the old-fashioned way—face-to-face with another person, without electronic devices.

Research aside, if you've ever felt the deep satisfaction of helping another person, making them smile, and giving them comfort, ease, and joy, you will appreciate what I'm saying. People who actively seek out ways to be helpful just feel better about themselves. They experience a "helper's high," a feeling of personal satisfaction that has been compared to an endorphin rush, and they feel less isolated and more connected. The bonus is that volunteers provide critical services that would  otherwise cost a tremendous amount of money, contributing to the economy and the public good. Volunteers improve the lives of others and strengthen our communities while experiencing great personal rewards. It's a win-win-win.

Taking the Next Step

Now that you have a little inspiration, or at least a spark of curiosity about how you can incorporate service and acts of kindness into your busy life, here are some instructions on how to use this book.

I believe that every person has something to give, and the many suggestions, tips, and ideas shared in *Simple Acts* will prove it. Whether you have a little time, a lot of energy, a new idea, a special talent, a few extra dollars (or the ability to fundraise), or the passion to rally others, you have something valuable and meaningful to give the world.

What You Will Find in These Pages

Each chapter in *Simple Acts* begins with background information. I share research, quotes, or interesting facts from experts in a related field to help you understand what is discussed. Then the chapter dives into specific tips, ideas, and resources. These include the websites of reputable national and international nonprofits that are working in the field, as well as suggestions for how you might connect with local community-based organizations doing this important work. I provide lots of ideas for how you can use your time, talents, and passions to be of service to the people around you, in all of the various communities you call home. You'll find sidebars sprinkled throughout the book that provide definitions, clarifying information, simple instructions, inspiring stories, websites of relevant organizations, and suggestions for ways you can "stretch" beyond routine community service if you are inspired to do more. My goal is always to provide you with simple, actionable, hands-on tools to make service and acts of kindness a part of your busy life.

A NOTE ABOUT ORGANIZATION MISSION AND VALUES

In my attempt to include a wide variety of resources, organizations, and websites for you to explore, best efforts were made to ensure that the organizations I suggest throughout *Simple Acts* are reputable, trustworthy, and doing good work in the communities they serve. Some of the organizations may be religiously affiliated, while others could support a particular political or philosophical viewpoint. You should always understand the history, mission, and values of the organizations you support with your time, interest, and donations and be sure that your values align with theirs. In the same way that you are an informed consumer about where (and by whom) your clothing is made or your food is grown, you should be an informed volunteer and supporter. For some suggestions on how to learn these details about an organization, check out the section titled "Making Sure an Organization Is Trustworthy" in chapter 1.

Chapter-By-Chapter Overview

Here is a brief description of what you'll find in *Simple Acts*:

Chapter 1: What's Your *Why*? The first chapter begins with a quiz—I promise, you don't need to study for it! It will help you identify issues you care about, and the rest of the chapter will teach you how to find trustworthy organizations to work with and suggest various ways to make a difference, both at home and at school.

Chapter 2: Don't Count the Hours; Make the Hours Count: This chapter discusses school-based community service requirements and service-learning programs and how those might inspire you to volunteer on your own. It includes resources so you can find meaningful service opportunities in your community and tips to help you make the most out of the experiences.

Chapter 3: Elevate Your Celebration: This chapter encourages you to acknowledge and celebrate special moments and milestones in your life with kindness, gratitude, and giving back.

Chapter 4: Finding the *Fun* in Fundraising: Raising money and awareness for a cause you care about is an important way that you can make an impact, and while fundraising can be hard work, you and your friends can also have fun doing it. You'll find lots of unique fundraising ideas in this chapter.

Chapter 5: Doing Well by Doing Good: This chapter introduces you to the concept of social entrepreneurship: running a business or other enterprise that gives back to the community while also creating a brand, selling a product, and making a profit.

Chapter 6: Turn Time *Off* **into Time** *On*: Your time off from school should be fun and relaxing, but it can also be filled with opportunities to learn, lead, grow, and give back, enriching your life and helping your community. This chapter covers information on internships, community service projects, and leadership opportunities that you can take on while you're on school breaks.

Chapter 7: #BeKind: As a "digital native," your life has always had technology and social media in it. This chapter encourages you to harness your digital skills and savvy to spread positivity, amplify important messages, and share stories of kindness.

Chapter 8: Not-So-Random Acts of Kindness: There are countless ways to be kind in your day-to-day life. *Simple Acts* concludes with a list of 52 intentional acts of kindness—one for every week of the year—to help you kick-start a lifelong kindness practice.

Visual Aids to Help You Find What You Are Looking For

Everything in *Simple Acts* falls into one or more of the following categories. Each category corresponds to its own unique icon so you can easily spot ideas that interest you. Look for the icons at the top of the page as you're flipping through the book. Hopefully, the ideas presented here will help you:

COLLECT AND DONATE: Many of us have stuff lying around— clothing, books, toys—that we've outgrown or no longer use, and we may not have anyone to pass them along to in our own family. Donating these things, or setting up a collection to encourage others to do so, is an easy way to give back. You can collect winter coats for children living in poverty, socks for people who are homeless, canned goods for a local food pantry—the list is endless. Organizing a collection and donating material goods costs nothing (or very little) and is a tangible way to help others while reducing waste through reuse and recycling. In later chapters, I provide instructions and tips on organizing collection drives.

EXPRESS GRATITUDE: I'm not going to bore you with reminders to say please and thank you, but I do suggest that we could all show a little more appreciation for all of the good things in our lives. Studies have shown that acknowledging and expressing gratitude (by simply writing down three things that you are thankful for each day) lowers stress, decreases depression, and increases optimism. The benefits are even greater when we express gratitude directly to the people we're thanking. Grateful people are just happier people. For me, one of the main motivations for doing service work is my own appreciation for the opportunities and comforts I am lucky enough to enjoy. So, in every setting and with each experience, start from a place of gratitude.

 LEARN ABOUT THE ISSUES THROUGH RESEARCH: Throughout this book, you'll learn that the only way to arm yourself with the knowledge you need to make an impact is to do the research, either online or by asking questions of the people and organizations that are actually doing the work. You've heard the phrase "knowledge is power," and it's certainly true when it comes to figuring out how you can tackle the difficult challenges facing the world. A word of caution, though—don't rely on social media and late-night comedians to get all of your information on an issue. Do your own research with reliable sources, ask good questions of trusted adults, and keep your ears open for unbiased and knowledgeable voices. There are also suggestions throughout this book for additional books you can read and resources you can explore to learn more about the topics being discussed.

 MAKE TIME TO VOLUNTEER: This is probably the toughest issue, and it's the primary reason I wrote this book. Teenagers are very busy, and finding time to give back in your community will usually mean *making* time, perhaps by saying no to some things in order to say yes to this. I hope *Simple Acts* will show you some manageable ways to do this in your busy life. In the following chapters, there are resources that will help you identify volunteer opportunities in your community and suggestions for ways you can give back in an informal way as you move through your day-to-day life. And there's information on remote or virtual volunteering, for times when it is very difficult or unsafe to volunteer in person.

NOTICE WHEN OTHERS ARE IN NEED: Keep your eyes open to those around you who may need help, listen (without judgment) when they are telling you their stories, and ask questions to learn more and better understand how you can be of service. Then, take the next step and *do* something. Even the smallest action can make the biggest impact.

 PAY IT FORWARD: This is a super simple concept: if someone does something nice for you, if you are the recipient of something good, think of a way to share that goodness with somebody else. Imagine what a huge difference it would make in the world if everyone else did this. Just remember this phrase: we rise by lifting others.

 RAISE MONEY AND AWARENESS: There's a whole chapter in *Simple Acts* about fundraising because it's important to understand that while most nonprofit organizations welcome your time, energy, and donated goods, what they *really* need is money. Young people have the energy and persistence that fundraising requires, and there are many people who have the financial resources and desire to make monetary contributions to good causes. We'll talk about ways to harness your unique abilities and your passion for doing good to raise critical resources for organizations and people who need them.

 SHARE YOUR IDEAS, SKILLS, AND CREATIVITY: Maybe you look around your neighborhood and see that your local playground is in disrepair, or you are sick of all of the food waste and plastic containers in your school cafeteria. You want to do something to fix these problems. You are creative, you have good ideas, you have skills—whether those are in using technology or building something with your hands—so you should feel empowered to approach leaders in your school and community to propose solutions. Your suggestions are valuable, but they can only bring change if you have the courage to articulate them clearly and share them with others.

It's important to note: **You don't need to read this book cover to cover.** You may want to jump around, since different chapters and topics may appeal to you at different times. The goal of the book is to meet you where you are at any given moment and nudge you toward taking the next step. Also, *Simple Acts* is not exhaustive, meaning I couldn't possibly include every service opportunity in every place. Every person will bring their own perspectives and preferences to this work, and every community and organization that is being served is different. You and your family know best what will work for you and what the people in your community need most urgently, understanding that those needs might change at any time. That's why it is so important to stay open and observant and to approach every person and situation with a positive attitude, a smile, and a genuine desire to help. I hope *Simple Acts* will be a useful tool, offering some new ideas and insights that you hadn't considered as you embark on a lifetime of kindness and purpose.

Whether You're Ready or Not, We Need You

Throughout history, the voices of young people have often been the loudest in raising alarms, demanding change, and leading the way.

As a young person, you are not only the future; you are the present. You're here now, reminding adults that today's problems won't magically go away unless adults work together to solve them, and that these problems will negatively impact your life if we don't address them. In my experience, teens speak with honesty and urgency about race, identity, sexuality, the environment, fairness, equity, and inclusion. They face challenges head-on with idealism and hope, and everyone should be watching and listening. I know that I am.

You may feel unprepared for all of this or overwhelmed by the pressure to "be the change you wish to see." Whether you know it or not, you have what you need to step into your role to make a difference.

Maybe you haven't yet fully identified your unique talents and gifts, the ones that we need you to share, but they do exist, waiting to come out and shine. Every single person, no matter who they are or where they live, how they were raised or what they believe, how much money or time they have, whether they have power or a platform—*everyone* has something to give. Remember: kindness costs nothing, and it is a choice you can make. Your job as an emerging adult is to figure out what you can offer by tapping into your interests and skills and keeping your eyes, ears, mind, and heart open to the possibilities. If you intentionally look for ways to be of service, you will find them, and your life and the lives of many others will be better for it. Young people continue to amaze and inspire me. I hope this book will inspire you to engage in simple acts of kindness as the building blocks of a purposeful life.

What's Your Why?

Identifying Your Passion and Finding Ways to Help

Ask yourself a few questions: What are your favorite activities or sports? What is your best subject in school, and why? What are your hobbies, passions, talents, and skills? These don't have to be organized activities like teams or performance groups. Maybe you easily connect with little kids, or you are physically strong, or you don't bore easily while doing monotonous tasks. You're good at something, and probably *lots* of things.

Now let's take a broader view. What concerns you most about the big issues facing your family, your community, your school, or your town? What worries you about the future of your country or our planet? What gets you fired up? What seems unfair? What makes you angry or sad?

Finally, what do you think you can do to help with any of these problems? I know this last question is a tough one, but if you had to brainstorm a few ideas, what would they be?

Human rights activist Archbishop Desmond Tutu famously said, "Do your little bit of good where you are; it's those little bits of good put together that overwhelm the world." This chapter helps you start to figure out what your little bits of good are and how to find organizations and people in your community that can benefit from them.

Let's think about some broad definitions of *community* and *service*. Imagine the concept of community as a series of concentric circles with you at the center. Your family, your caregivers, or the people with whom you are living at this time are the innermost ring of your community. Your acts of service start in your home in relation to these people. Your family may be counting on you to help out in lots of different ways: caring for younger siblings or aging grandparents, running errands, doing laundry, preparing meals, taking out the trash. These may sound like chores, but everything you are doing is important work and should be valued as a contribution to the common good.

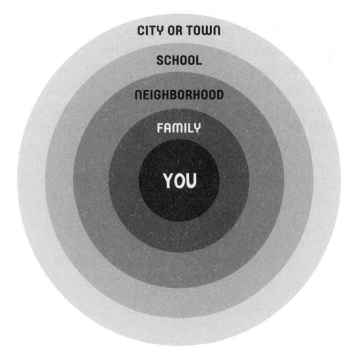

Next, there is service that you do for the people who live in your neighborhood. You hold the door open for an elderly or disabled person in your apartment building, pick up litter when you see it, or clear the snow from a neighbor's front porch. Your school community is also counting on you in many ways: to be a good and kind class-mate, to help when you see others struggling, to do your part in keeping your school safe. Your city or town expects you to follow the laws, help keep public spaces clean, and support your local food pantry or community kitchen if you are able. Whether you recognize it as service or not, you are serving others all the time in your day-to-day life, so you should feel pretty good about that.

Now let's widen the lens a bit and think about people and issues a little further outside of your day-to-day experience. There are plenty of ways to make a difference for people you don't know and will likely never meet. The mission of many national and international organizations is to have broad impact, and it's possible for you to become a member, learn more, and give back through them.

As you begin to think about the ways that you define community and the issues that you care about, let's take a moment to drill down a little deeper. On page 15, take a brief quiz that will help you identify your strengths and the best ways that you can use your talents and skills to help others. Don't overthink it—just answer honestly and thoughtfully. Your likes, dislikes, strengths, and challenges are the subject of this quiz, and you know yourself best. Hopefully, once you've completed the quiz, you'll have a deeper understanding of the unique tools that are in your personal toolbox and the ways that you can make the most impact. Then, you can keep these in mind as you read through *Simple Acts* and let the icons point you toward the best opportunities for YOU.

What's in My Toolbox?

Self-Assessment

1. How do you approach new people and situations?

  A. I'm a little shy and hesitant; I usually hang back and observe.

  B. I'm an outgoing people person. I jump right in.

  C. I learn by doing and am usually comfortable meeting and working with others who are doing the same activities as me.

  D. I may start off slow, but if I feel comfortable or I'm with friends, I'm more likely to engage.

2. How would you describe your talents?

  A. I'm curious and organized, and I like learning and doing research.

  B. I'm a great teacher. I like making friends and sharing what I'm passionate about.

  C. I'm creative and artistic, and I love to share my talents with others.

  D. I don't really know what I have to offer, but I'm excited to figure it out.

3. How would you describe your abilities?

  A. I'm a hard worker but would rather stay behind the scenes a bit.

  B. I'm confident and can put others at ease or help them understand new concepts.

  C. I'm a hands-on person; I like to get my hands "dirty" doing a task.

  D. I'm willing to try new things.

4. How do you handle rejection and difficult situations?

  A. I'm a little sensitive; I'm reluctant to put myself out there.

  B. I'm not easily offended; I can brush off rejection and start over.

continued ❯

What's in My Toolbox?

    C. I like to get feedback and critiques on my work but struggle with outright rejection or having others angry with me.

    D. I'm usually resilient, especially if I'm with friends who can support me.

5. Are you able to easily name the issues you care about?

    A. There are lots of issues that make me curious, sad, or angry, but I don't really know how I can help.

    B. I know exactly what gets me fired up, and I'm anxious to get out there and start working to make a difference.

    C. The specific issues are less important to me as long as I can share my talents through meaningful work.

    D. I don't really know what issues are impacting people in my community or how I can help, but I'm open to learning.

If you answered mostly **As**, you are a thoughtful information seeker. You might not gravitate toward in-person or hands-on volunteer opportunities right off the bat, but you can still make a big impact on your community and the world. You're more likely to research and learn about issues before jumping in. You might enjoy virtual service opportunities that allow you to help from a distance or kitchen table kindness activities. If you are drawn to political activism and social justice issues, you might be the person who organizes behind the scenes, who sets up the petition, and who sends out information about letter-writing campaigns. Instead of shouting from rooftops, asking for donations or volunteering in person, you might prefer to manage the social media account for the club, organization, or nonprofit you're working with; order necessary supplies; send email reminders; and do the important follow-up.

If you answered mostly **Bs**, you are probably well suited for in-person volunteering and fundraising efforts. Your ability to dive into a new situation and to interact comfortably (and respectfully) with different

What's in My Toolbox?

people means that you will be willing to try new volunteer opportunities that might be outside of your typical comfort zone. Because you are a people person, you might notice the needs of others more easily. Perhaps you'll realize you have a knack for fundraising. As you'll learn in chapter 4, having the courage to ask for donations on behalf of a worthy cause is a gift, as is the ability to stay motivated and positive when people say no. Your outgoing personality will serve you well in leading your peers in volunteer outings, rallying around service events in your school, and approaching new or challenging tasks with a can-do attitude.

If you answered mostly **Cs**, you enjoy hands-on work. You may be reserved and shy, very outgoing, or somewhere in between, but as long as you have a task or project to work on, you're comfortable both being with people and working alone. You might find yourself crafting items to donate, using your artistic skills to create posters, or planting a tree. If you have a specific talent, you might even find organizations looking for people with your skill set! Not all organizations and nonprofits have hands-on work all the time, but your adaptability will help you push yourself outside of your comfort zone occasionally when you need to. Your creativity and your ability to pick up new things quickly as you do them will help you in any volunteering situation.

If you answered mostly **Ds**, maybe you've never volunteered before. If that's the case, your initial hesitation or uncertainty is totally understandable. The important thing is your open-mindedness and willingness to learn and try. You are a person who should absolutely find peers who care about the same issues that you do. Then, make an effort to volunteer together as a group. Everything is easier and more fun when done with others, and you are more likely to continue the work if you are with people who are just as enthusiastic and committed as you are. Use the resources in this book to identify the issues that concern you, and then connect with peers, teachers, community volunteers, or family members to work together toward a solution.

continued ›

┌─ What's in My Toolbox? ──────────────────

What Do You Really Care About? List All That Apply

This list will help you identify the people and issues that really tug at your heart and spark your curiosity. No judgment here—check only the ones that you really care about. You'll be able to keep this list in mind and refer back to it as you read through the book and find suggestions for ways to learn about, volunteer for, or fundraise for a particular cause or issue.

I really care about / worry for / get upset about:

- ☐ Animals (pets)
- ☐ Animals (wildlife)
- ☐ Children/adults who are living with illnesses or disabilities
- ☐ Children/families living in poverty or dealing with economic inequality
- ☐ Children/teens navigating the foster care system
- ☐ Discrimination and inequality (in all forms)
- ☐ Educational disparities
- ☐ The environment / climate change / maintaining our green spaces
- ☐ Finding cures for illness and disease
- ☐ Food waste
- ☐ Global poverty
- ☐ Gun violence
- ☐ Isolated seniors and elderly people who need help with day-to-day tasks
- ☐ Natural disaster relief
- ☐ People experiencing hunger or food insecurity
- ☐ People experiencing housing insecurity or homelessness

What's in My Toolbox?

- ❏ Public health concerns (raising awareness around the importance of exercise, a healthy diet, vaccines, and organ donation, as well as the dangers of drugs, alcohol, vaping and cigarettes, and so on)
- ❏ Spreading kindness generally
- ❏ Voting rights

Finally, the "Good List"

Quickly (without thinking too much—off the top of your head) write down EVERYTHING you are good at doing. Don't just list things that people typically call "talents," like singing, drawing, or playing a musical instrument. List it all! Are you patient? Can you do complicated math problems easily? Are you physically strong? Do you like to organize things? Is your handwriting neat? Are you a good driver? Do you have a loud voice? Are you funny? Are you good with young kids? Go ahead and brag about yourself a little bit. I hope you'll be pleasantly surprised by the number of things you have on your list. Keep it handy as you read through the book—first, as a reminder of how amazing you are, but also as a resource. And don't hesitate to add to the list later on! When you have an idea for a cause that you care about, pull out this list and see if there is something here—a skill, talent, or ability—that you can share to make an impact on that issue.

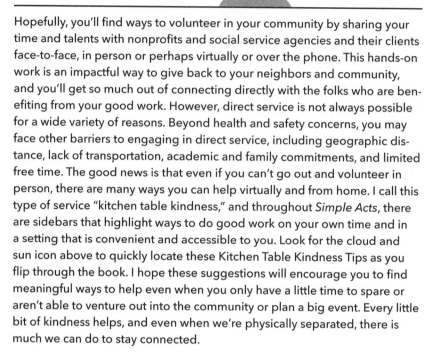

KITCHEN TABLE KINDNESS TIP

Hopefully, you'll find ways to volunteer in your community by sharing your time and talents with nonprofits and social service agencies and their clients face-to-face, in person or perhaps virtually or over the phone. This hands-on work is an impactful way to give back to your neighbors and community, and you'll get so much out of connecting directly with the folks who are benefiting from your good work. However, direct service is not always possible for a wide variety of reasons. Beyond health and safety concerns, you may face other barriers to engaging in direct service, including geographic distance, lack of transportation, academic and family commitments, and limited free time. The good news is that even if you can't go out and volunteer in person, there are many ways you can help virtually and from home. I call this type of service "kitchen table kindness," and throughout *Simple Acts*, there are sidebars that highlight ways to do good work on your own time and in a setting that is convenient and accessible to you. Look for the cloud and sun icon above to quickly locate these Kitchen Table Kindness Tips as you flip through the book. I hope these suggestions will encourage you to find meaningful ways to help even when you only have a little time to spare or aren't able to venture out into the community or plan a big event. Every little bit of kindness helps, and even when we're physically separated, there is much we can do to stay connected.

Making Sure an Organization Is Trustworthy

As you read through this chapter and identify the causes that you care about and the types of volunteer work you'd like to do, you'll need to find organizations to help. *Simple Acts* will point you toward some reputable national organizations that have been operating for a long time and are worthy of your time. Many of these will allow you to search for local affiliates. You'll also want to identify trustworthy organizations based in your own community. Keeping your eyes and ears open is sometimes the best way to find these opportunities—you may hear about things from friends, classmates, and trusted adults who volunteer. Pay attention to social media posts sharing positive service experiences, notice flyers hanging in coffee shops, and be aware of upcoming events on your school or community calendar.

Next, you'll want to research (or "vet") the organizations that you are interested in helping. Use the following steps to check whether a particular organization is the right fit for you:

- Navigate around the organization's website (if there is one). Does it offer specific information about how to volunteer, the types of volunteer activities, and whom to contact for more information? Does it include testimonials from other volunteers? Do they welcome young volunteers? Understand the rules around age requirements and whether you'll need permission from a parent or guardian or need to be accompanied by an adult if you are under 18.

- Check to see if the organization you are exploring is rated by Charity Navigator (charitynavigator.org), GuideStar (guidestar .org), or GreatNonprofits (greatnonprofits.org). These rating organizations use criteria to ensure that nonprofits are meeting their stated missions, utilizing donated funds appropriately, reporting their finances to the government, and providing quality volunteer opportunities. A positive rating is a good indication that the organization is well managed, effective in achieving its mission, worth your time, and deserving of your donations.

- Follow the organization on social media, and pay attention to the tone and content of its posts. Are the posts well-written (without inappropriate language), positive, and supportive of the clients they serve? Do the posts celebrate and show gratitude to their volunteers and donors? Does the organization amplify and share important information about the issues it addresses? Check out the number and types of followers and the comments they write. Make sure these are in line with your values. Chapter 7 will dive deeper into the power of social media to spread positive messages and promote service.

- Identify a volunteer coordinator or an executive director at the organization, and contact them to ask questions about the types of volunteer opportunities available and any training being provided. Notice how quickly the organization responds to your inquiry and how forthcoming it is with information. This will give you a sense of the mission and culture and whether it is a place where you will feel welcome and comfortable.

- Be sure that the organization's mission—which may be stated on an "Our Mission" or "About Us" page on its website or in its social media bio—is in line with your values and that the work you will be doing matches your interests.

- If you'd like to dive a little deeper, check the website to see if the annual report is posted there. If so, download it and read it thoroughly. If you can't find an annual report online, you can ask the organization to provide one. If it is a reputable charitable organization and is identified by the government as a 501(c)(3) (tax-exempt organization), it should provide a detailed report to donors and members of the community who provide support. This research will give you a sense of the financial stability of the organization, how it raises and uses funds, and the strength of the leaders who are managing the operation.

- Finally, I'd like to share a popular slogan: "Nothing about us without us." This means that no policy should be decided by any organization or governing body without the participation of members of the group affected by that policy. This concept shows the importance of representation and highlights the need for everyone to have a voice around issues that directly impact them. The slogan is especially connected to the disability rights movement. This is the movement for people with disabilities to have full participation in policies that affect them and to have equal opportunities. When considering this slogan in the context of selecting a nonprofit to support, try to find out how the people being served by an organization have a say in its operation. The leadership, staff, and volunteers should be people who adequately reflect (and therefore understand) the identity, history, and experience of the individuals or groups being served.

This chapter uses the icons for different categories of giving back to help you identify issues and opportunities that appeal to you without too much searching. The problem or social justice issue is listed at the top of each section, followed by:

- ways you can get involved in person, at home, or in your school;

- suggestions on how to find local organizations in your own community that need your help; and

- names of national or international organizations you can research and support.

Issues You Might Be Passionate About

Hunger and Food Insecurity

According to the United States Department of Agriculture (USDA), it is estimated that over 35 million people, including 11 million children, in the United States were "food insecure" in 2019. This means millions of people lived in households that had inconsistent access to enough food for all household members. The pandemic and resulting unemployment and financial crisis of 2020 likely increased those numbers significantly. As of March 2021, Feeding America estimated that 45 million people—1 in 7—experienced food insecurity in 2020. These numbers are always changing. Take a moment to **RESEARCH** the current state of food insecurity in the United States at the USDA's Economic Research Service (ers.usda.gov/topics/food -nutrition-assistance) and in the world at the World Bank's Food Security page (worldbank.org/en/topic/food-security). As these pages help demonstrate, hunger is an enormous problem, one that has devastating consequences for millions of people and is especially frustrating because of the amount of food that is wasted every day.

Households with children are more likely to experience food insecurity, and every community in the United States has families who struggle with this issue. Whether you realize it or not, you have seen the face of hunger in your neighborhood and in your school, regardless of where you live. There are many nonprofits that focus on feeding hungry people, and there are lots of ways that you can help make sure that everyone has their basic need for nourishment met. **MAKE TIME TO VOLUNTEER** in your local food bank, food pantry, or community kitchen.

Don't know where to find it? Search your zip code on one of the following databases:

- Ample Harvest (ampleharvest.org)
- Feeding America (feedingamerica.org/find-your-local-foodbank)
- Food Finder (foodfinder.us)
- Food Pantries (foodpantries.org)
- Homeless Shelter Directory (homelessshelterdirectory.org)
- Department of Housing and Urban Development Find Shelter (hud.gov/findshelter)
- SoupKitchen411 (soupkitchen411.com)

SHARING MORE THAN A MEAL

If you are volunteering at a community kitchen, you will likely be asked to do specific tasks, like set up tables and chairs, prepare or serve food, wash trays, sweep, and clean up. If you have a talent, like playing the guitar, singing, doing card tricks, or juggling, consider asking the volunteer coordinator if you can also **SHARE YOUR TALENT** and entertain the guests during the meal service. The joy you will spread will be just as welcome as the food.

MAKE TIME TO VOLUNTEER delivering prepared meals through a Meals on Wheels program or collecting leftover food through a food rescue organization.

- Find the local affiliate of the national Meals on Wheels program by searching the website (mealsonwheelsamerica.org). Look for other private nonprofits, including faith-based organizations, working to deliver hot meals to your homebound ill and elderly neighbors.

- Food "rescue" or recovery is the practice of collecting prepared, untouched food from events and restaurants and delivering it immediately to people who are hungry. **RESEARCH** your local food rescue organizations to learn more about volunteer opportunities through the following links:
  ◇ Feeding America (feedingamerica.org)
  ◇ Food Recovery Network (foodrecoverynetwork.org)
  ◇ Food Rescue Locator (foodrescuelocator.com)
  ◇ National Gleaning Project (nationalgleaningproject.org)

KITCHEN TABLE KINDNESS TIP:
SENDING LOVE TO ISOLATED SENIORS

Explore the websites of your local Meals on Wheels and other food delivery programs. These organizations may encourage volunteers to create colorful notes of encouragement, birthday cards, holiday cards, decorated paper place mats, or delivery bags. These items brighten food delivery packages around holidays and on client birthdays, and they're a great way for volunteers who can't participate directly in preparing, packaging, or delivering food to engage with the organizations.

When you are heading out to the grocery store for your own family, **NOTICE** if an elderly or ill neighbor is homebound and, if it is within your budget to do so, reach out to ask if they are in need of anything.

Host a food **COLLECTION DRIVE** at your school, house of worship, or community center, and donate collected items to your local food pantry.

HOW TO ORGANIZE A COLLECTION DRIVE

Nonperishable food drives are common around the Thanksgiving holiday, but of course, hunger and food insecurity impact people every day of the year. Collection drives give everyone an opportunity to participate even if they don't have a lot of disposable income to donate. Donors do not necessarily need to purchase new items—they likely have a can of soup or box of pasta in their own pantry at home that they can spare and would be happy to share with someone in need. If you are collecting other items, like gently used clothing, books, toys, or sports equipment, you are giving your donors an opportunity to sort through their own closets for items that have been outgrown or replaced.

There are a few simple steps to organizing a successful collection drive:

◇ Get permission from the school administration or the management of the location where you will be hosting the donation drive.

◇ Understand the specific need you are trying to fill. If you are collecting nonperishable food items, contact the food pantry to be sure they will accept donated items and to check exactly which kinds of foods they need. The same is true for clothing, toys, books, or any other items you are collecting. Know what is needed, and try to fill that need.

◇ Set up large, sturdy boxes for collection. Ask local moving and storage companies if they can donate boxes for this effort.

◇ Decorate the boxes or hang signs from them to generate interest and excitement. Be clear about the specific items being collected and the deadline for all donations.

◇ Recruit volunteers for the pickup and delivery of the collected items, preferably people with access to vehicles to help with transportation. Ask for volunteers from moving, storage, or trucking companies, or recruit individuals with minivans or trucks. This effort needs to be organized well in advance to ensure that all donations are handled appropriately and deliveries are coordinated and timely.

FUNDRAISE for international, national, and local organizations that fight hunger. There are lots of details around how to raise money for a cause in chapter 4 to help make your fundraising efforts a success. Some hunger organizations provide detailed instructions and fundraising campaign materials on their websites. A few to explore:

- Bread for the World Institute (bread.org)
- Feeding America (feedingamerica.org)
- Food for the Hungry (fh.org)
- Heifer International (heifer.org)
- The Hunger Project (thp.org)
- No Kid Hungry (nokidhungry.org)

Service in School

Hunger and food insecurity very likely impact your classmates, staff and others associated with your school, and people living in your neighborhood, town, or city. Talking about hunger, and making sure that people who are in need of help do not feel ashamed or marginalized, is important. Food is a basic human right, and everyone should have access to adequate nutrition. One in six kids in the United States doesn't know where their next meal is coming from, and many rely on school-based meals for nutrition. Students who come to school hungry have difficulty concentrating, have more social and behavioral problems, and are more likely to repeat grades. If this is an issue you care about, there is action you can take. In addition to hosting a **FOOD DRIVE** or **FUNDRAISING** event as mentioned above, you can mobilize classmates to work with the administration of your school and the Department of Education in your area to be sure that school-based meals are accessible, that food waste is minimized, and that leftover food is donated to food rescue organizations as appropriate. If your school allows students to make presentations on important topics, you can speak to your classmates about the issue of hunger in your community. If you're interested in political activism, you can mobilize friends to write letters and call your local representatives to be sure that funding is being given to local food pantries and that SNAP (food stamp) benefits remain intact when budget cuts inevitably threaten them. The Feeding America website provides clear, actionable steps you can take, including signing a pledge (feedingamerica.org/take-action/advocate/campaign-to-end-hunger) to stand with your community and speak out against hunger.

Poverty and Economic Injustice

As of 2019, the poverty rate in the United States is estimated to be 10.5 percent, and the percentage of children living in poverty is even higher, at 17 percent. The World Bank estimated in 2017 that 9.2 percent of the global population, or 689 million people, live in extreme poverty (which means they live on less than $1.90 per day). People often transition in and out of poverty depending on whether they have a job, their health and marital status, and the stability of their housing, among other factors. Many families struggle financially on an ongoing basis and have difficulty having enough money for food, clothing, rent, and utilities. Social service agencies—public governmental agencies and private nonprofits—provide services and resources for those experiencing financial hardship, and many of these organizations would welcome your help.

RESEARCH organizations in your community that are providing assistance to people living in poverty. This work may include a wide range of services, including educational opportunities or employment counseling; assistance with filling out forms and applying for aid; or providing items like diapers and formula for new parents, books and supplies for underfunded schools, or coats for children in need of warm clothing.

Once you've identified an organization to help, offer to sponsor a **COLLECTION DRIVE**. Be sure to listen carefully so that you are collecting the items that are needed most. You can collect from individuals and families, but you might also consider asking local small businesses as well as large corporations to donate items in bulk. For example, you might **NOTICE** that a local clothing vendor throws out-of-season clothing in a bargain bin before discarding it or shipping it back to the manufacturer. You can approach the store owner and tell them about the nonprofit you are supporting and ask if they might be willing to donate some of the old merchandise. The logistics of collection drives can be complicated, so recruit some friends to do it with you. You'll need to set up collection boxes, promote the effort, set a deadline, and figure out how to transport all of the donated items to the organization.

DIAPER NEED

One in three American families struggles with diaper need. Disposable diapers are very expensive, and many families simply can't afford to purchase the many diapers that babies need before they are toilet trained. Families may be forced to make the impossible choice between buying food or buying diapers, and some parents may reuse dirty diapers, leading to rashes and other health problems for babies. There are many organizations that are working to fight diaper need, and you can find one in your community with the National Diaper Bank Network directory (nationaldiaperbanknetwork.org/member-directory). Setting up a diaper **COLLECTION** is a great way to help families struggling with this problem.

If you are organizing a clothing drive, you'll have an opportunity to start in your own closet and **PAY IT FORWARD**. Perhaps you've been the recipient of a coat, a pair of shoes, or a sweatshirt that you loved (and for which you were **GRATEFUL**) but you've now outgrown. If you can't pass it down to someone in your own family, consider donating it to a local organization. At the change of seasons or at the end of each school year, make an effort to sort through your gently used things and be sure to **DONATE** the items that are still in good condition. A quick internet search may help you identify local social service agencies and homeless or domestic violence shelters that would accept gently used clothing or outerwear. Many national organizations have local affiliates in communities across the country, and their websites allow you to locate the branch in your area. The nonprofit Dress for Success (dressforsuccess.org) collects gently used professional clothing and accessories. The American Red Cross has partnered with an organization called GreenDrop (gogreendrop .com) to create clothing donation bins and schedule at-home pickups. Goodwill is one established nonprofit that will also gladly accept donations, and you can find a local collection box by searching its website (goodwill.org).

If you are interested in making sure that every child has a warm coat in the winter, check out Operation Warm (operationwarm.org) or One Warm Coat (onewarmcoat.org), nonprofits that can help you organize a coat collection drive and will identify an organization in your community to receive the coats and distribute them to children in need.

RESEARCH and educate yourself about the national and global issues that impact poverty and about ways you can become involved with reputable organizations making an impact. These include:

- CARE (care.org)
- The Children's Defense Fund (childrensdefense.org)
- ONE (one.org)
- Oxfam (oxfam.org)
- Save the Children (savethechildren.org)
- UNICEF (unicef.org)
- World Vision (worldvision.org)

Service in School

Issues like generational poverty or economic injustice may seem too big to wrap your arms around, and you might wonder what you can do to help. This is where knowledge is power. In a school setting, you have the benefit of teachers—in a variety of subjects, including history, economics, and social studies—who can suggest books to read on the subject and who can lead discussions for students who are interested in learning more about the complex causes of poverty. Who knows? This process might help you decide to become a teacher as you realize that education is a powerful tool in helping people pull themselves out of poverty. Or you might plan to study law so that you can fight for economic justice and fairness. Of course, those are big things regarding your future dreams, but school is also the perfect place to brainstorm small ways to make a meaningful difference in the lives of people who are struggling in your community. You can pick one activity—for example, **COLLECTING** new toys and holiday gifts for children living in poverty—and set up a collection drive at school to meet that need. This effort may not solve generational poverty, but it is real and tangible. You can provide joy to children and relief to their parents during the holiday season. Never underestimate the power of small gestures.

Homelessness

According to the US Department of Housing and Urban development, about 18 out of every 10,000 people experience homelessness on any given night in the United States. The majority (nearly 70 percent) of these folks are individuals, and the remainder are families with children. While the perception of homelessness is that it only occurs in big cities, in reality, it touches people in many suburban and rural communities as well. The basic need for shelter—a place to sleep, eat your meals, and feel safe—is often out of reach for people experiencing poverty, job loss, domestic abuse, or mental illness, among other challenges. Homelessness is a complicated issue with no quick fix, but there are many good resources online where you can learn more about the problem and how you can help.

WORDS ARE IMPORTANT

The words we use to describe a social justice issue—and the people affected by it—are very important, and they set a tone for how we treat people experiencing hardship. A person who is currently living on the street or in a shelter is not a "homeless person"; they are experiencing homelessness or living marginally. Another term you might consider using is *unhoused,* which signifies that a person may have a home they're temporarily or indefinitely unable to live in. Or it may indicate that a person considers their current form of shelter (which may be a homeless shelter, tent city, or other non-traditional dwelling) to be home even if they don't have a house. Similarly, someone who is sick is not a "cancer victim" but rather a person living with a disease. A person is not "poor" or "needy"; they are struggling with financial hardship or working to overcome generational poverty. It's not that it's *inaccurate* to say someone is "a homeless person"—it's that it can be dehumanizing and diminishing to define someone by a circumstance or challenge in this way.

Using respectful language that puts the person before the situation allows people to retain their dignity and humanity, and it prevents us from othering them. We need to remember that we will all be in need of help one day. Each person we encounter deserves to be recognized as a complex, unique human being, worthy of our kindness and respect regardless of their current circumstances. The way we talk to them and about them should reflect this.

RESEARCH some of the excellent national organizations that are working to understand the problem of homelessness and to advocate for solutions:

- Goodwill (goodwill.org)
- National Alliance to End Homelessness (endhomelessness.org)
- National Coalition for the Homeless (nationalhomeless.org)
- StandUp for Kids (standupforkids.org)
- United Way (unitedway.org)
- YWCA (ywca.org)

MAKE TIME TO VOLUNTEER at a local homeless shelter. If you don't know where one is, search your zip code on the Homeless Shelter Directory (homelessshelterdirectory.org) or the US Department of Housing and Urban Development's Find Shelter tool (hud.gov/findshelter). You may be able to help with food preparation or service, shelter cleaning or maintenance, gathering or organizing donations, or other tasks.

You may also find street outreach organizations in your community that engage trained volunteers to visit areas of the city where people experiencing homelessness congregate. You can deliver sandwiches, toiletry kits, socks, and other essentials. Not all outreach organizations will allow teens under 18 to do street outreach work. And regardless of your age, it is important to work with an organization that is doing this work safely. You should always be accompanied by trained adults and receive proper training yourself. The United States Interagency Council on Homelessness (USICH) has created a helpful document called "Core Elements of Effective Street Outreach to People Experiencing Homelessness," which can be found on the USICH website (usich.gov) under the tab labeled "Tools for Action."

KITCHEN TABLE KINDNESS TIP: MADE WITH LOVE

If you are a person who loves to knit, crochet, or sew, you can create warm scarves, hats, or blankets for people who are living marginally or experiencing homelessness or for children living in shelters. As discussed elsewhere in this book, being crafty isn't simply a way for you to pass the time and express your **CREATIVITY**. You can make items that are functional and would be deeply appreciated by people who have fallen on hard times and may be feeling alone or unloved. Never underestimate how much a person who is facing challenges might be comforted by a handmade gift, something that is especially meaningful because of the time and care taken to create it. These things are a tangible manifestation of kindness and love.

Organize a **COLLECTION** of essential items like socks, long underwear, and toiletries. Work with a homelessness outreach organization to be sure you are collecting the items that are most needed and requested, as these types of items need to be new.

MEETING LESS OBVIOUS NEEDS

Those experiencing homelessness are in need of many things. Some things, like food, toiletries, and warm clothing, are obvious. However, as you think about all of the things you use on a daily basis and keep in your home, you will realize that people living on the street may need additional items, like sunscreen, bug spray, menstrual products, diapers for their children, toilet paper, eating utensils, first aid kits, underwear, and bedding. Working closely with a recipient agency will help you identify the most important items you can collect.

Service in School

In addition to the collection drives and other activities mentioned above, perhaps the most important things you can do for people living marginally, who are unhoused or experiencing homelessness, are to **LEARN** about the issues and to advocate for change in your community. The root causes of homelessness include many complex problems that are often layered on top of one another: domestic violence; addiction and recovery; job loss, underemployment, and lack of a living wage; mental health issues and inadequate mental health services; inequality, prejudice, and discrimination on the basis of race, gender, sexual identity, age, ability, nationality, immigration status, and more; and the rising cost of housing. The solution isn't as simple as providing a roof over someone's head, though certainly that helps! Whether you live in a city where homelessness is an issue or in a more rural area where poverty holds neighbors back from achieving their dreams, there is much to learn and discuss, and there is advocacy work that you can do. Consider organizing a discussion (or a series of talks) with your classmates, inviting speakers from the local government and social service agencies. Ask a history or social studies teacher or other faculty member to be a mentor and facilitator for your group. Understanding the issues will allow you to brainstorm meaningful ways you might work together on a solution, utilizing many other tools described in this book.

Education and Youth Enrichment

South African anti-apartheid revolutionary and former president Nelson Mandela believed that education is the most powerful weapon that can be used to change the world. Unfortunately, many children around the globe don't have access to a high-quality education or access to education at all. There are kids in your own community who don't have educational support at home, whether in the form of tutoring or mentoring or simply having a parent with enough time to help them with homework. Some kids may lack the basic supplies, like books, pencils, and notebooks, that are necessary to feel prepared to learn. A study by the National Center for Education Statistics found that 94 percent of public-school teachers (most of whom do not earn a high salary) pay for classroom supplies out of their own pockets. After-school enrichment classes are financially out of reach for many families, and programs focused on art, music, dance, and physical fitness are typically the first ones cut in public schools when budget money runs low. If you enjoy spending time with younger kids; if you have an interest in becoming a teacher; if you love music, dance, sports, or art; or if you just want to **EXPRESS GRATITUDE** and **PAY IT FORWARD** for the education you are receiving, there are many ways you can empower kids in your community and around the world.

SHARE YOUR CREATIVE TALENTS AND SKILLS.

- Use your skills as a tech-savvy digital native and offer to teach younger kids how to use the internet or word processing.

- If you know how to play a musical instrument or are trained in dance or musical theater, seek out an underresourced arts program in your community where you might be able to teach or assist.

- Physical fitness is so important for everyone, but especially for growing children. If you love playing a particular sport and think you have a strong understanding of the fundamentals of the game, volunteer to coach kids in an after-school program.

Organize a **COLLECTION DRIVE** of gently used sporting equipment to donate to your local Boys & Girls Club (bgca.org) or Big Brothers Big Sisters program (bbbs.org). National organizations that encourage collection drives and accept donations of sports equipment include:

- GOALS Haiti (goalshaiti.org)
- Let's Play It Forward (letsplayitforward.org)
- Peace Passers (peacepassers.org)
- Pitch In for Baseball & Softball (pifbs.org)

Starting school with a new backpack full of school supplies is a luxury that many children can't afford. Consider hosting a backpack-**COLLECTION DRIVE** in your community over the summer, or search for organizations already doing this work. Volunteers of America (voa.org/operation-backpack) hosts Operation Backpack in many cities around the United States.

DONATE your birthday (ask for donations instead of gifts for yourself) or host a **FUNDRAISING** drive for First Book (firstbook.org), an organization that aims to remove barriers to quality education by providing affordable resources like high-quality books, sports equipment, winter coats, and snacks to its member network of more than 500,000 educators.

RESEARCH nonprofit organizations that are making strides in bridging the gap in educational disparities around the United States, or identify international organizations addressing the lack of education for children living in poverty around the world. Some established organizations include:

- DonorsChoose (donorschoose.org)
- The Mr. Holland's Opus Foundation (mhopus.org)
- Pencils of Promise (pencilsofpromise.org)
- Reach Out and Read (reachoutandread.org)
- Save the Children (savethechildren.org)
- Teach for America (teachforamerica.org)

Service in School

At the start of the school year, host a bake sale **FUNDRAISER** in support of the #BakeAChange campaign for She's the First (shesthefirst.org /cupcakes), an organization that funds programs to educate and empower girls around the world.

You might also consider **VOLUNTEERING** to tutor a younger student in your school or at the middle or elementary school you attended. You can take this idea a step further and organize a pool of tutors from among your classmates. Post the list of volunteers and their available times on a district-wide web page serving public schools in your area, including charter schools; websites for specialized tutoring programs; and social service agencies' websites. Old-fashioned bulletin boards around your community are also a great way to spread the word. Tutoring need not mean teaching specific academic subjects, like math or science. It may just be reading aloud with young children or allowing them to read aloud to you. Taking the time to listen and patiently offering your help can make a huge difference in the life of a child who is struggling in school.

Isolated Seniors

Isolation, loneliness, and depression are common among the elderly, many of whom live alone and far away from family. Research has shown that 60 percent of seniors living in nursing homes receive NO visitors each year. The COVID-19 pandemic and subsequent quarantine for vulnerable elderly people, who were disproportionately affected by the disease, exacerbated this problem and brought it into the national spotlight. If you've spent time with an elderly relative, grandparent, or neighbor, you know that they have many stories to share. Intergenerational volunteering is a win-win. The older adult feels seen and heard, and if you open your heart with patience and kindness, you'll gain unexpected wisdom and perspective.

NOTICE the older folks who live in your apartment building, on your block, or around your neighborhood. Befriend them, greet them warmly, ask them questions about their lives, tell them about your day. If you notice that you haven't seen them in a while, check in on them. Offer to bring them coffee, a cold drink, or a meal. Pick up the newspaper that was thrown on their lawn and place it at the door. If you are heading out to the grocery store, ask them if they need anything. Clear their porch or walkway when it snows, spread salt when it is icy, rake the leaves. Loneliness and isolation often lead to depression and physical sickness, and this is especially so for elderly people who are homebound. Your friendship, care, and kindness can brighten a senior's day, helping them feel better mentally, emotionally, and physically.

MAKE TIME TO VOLUNTEER at a local senior center, assisted-living facility, nursing home, or senior outreach program. A quick internet search will help you identify senior housing in your community, or you can check the National Council on Aging website (ncoa.org) for a map of local senior centers it partners with.

Volunteering with seniors is usually focused on friendly visiting. The greatest gifts you can give to an isolated older adult are your time, attention, and kindness. Listening to stories, asking questions, and offering information about your own life help make a connection. Many senior-focused organizations create specific opportunities to interact with their clients, like bingo nights, chess tournaments, meal delivery events, or holiday parties. There's no limit to what you might offer. You can **SHARE** a musical **TALENT**, garden together, play cards, or teach a senior how to use their cell phone or computer to connect with distant family.

KITCHEN TABLE KINDNESS TIP:
SENDING LOVE TO ISOLATED SENIORS

You can write letters to isolated seniors and send them to organizations like Love for Our Elders (loveforourelders.org) or Letters Against Isolation (lettersagainstisolation.com).

If you are an artist, you can use your **CREATIVITY** to make cards, paper flowers, valentines, holiday decorations, or place mats for your local senior center or nursing home. Spending time drawing or crafting can also provide stress relief for you in your hectic life, and these are fun activities to do with friends, younger siblings, or kids you are babysitting.

Service in School

Intergenerational volunteering is important for the health and well-being of our elderly population, and it strengthens and connects communities. Forming a bond between your school and your elderly neighbors is a great way for you and your classmates to make a meaningful impact. With the help of school administrators, reach out to a local nursing home, adult day healthcare center, or senior services agency to ask if your school can partner with them for an entire school year. Recruit classmates and create a buddy program matching student volunteers with elderly neighbors for friendly visits or phone calls. There are many **CREATIVE** ways that your school can support your partner organization and the seniors who live or access services there. You can plan holiday gatherings and special events. For example, a group of students could spend an evening in December walking room to room singing Christmas carols, or you could organize a monthly bingo game, sing-along, or talent show. You can invite your new friends to an event you are already planning, like a pep rally, a theatrical presentation, or an arts festival, and teens who are able to drive can provide transportation to and from events. Elderly "buddies" with unique and compelling life stories—a veteran who served overseas, a Holocaust survivor, or someone who was politically active during the civil rights movement—can be invited to speak to classes studying these historical subjects. Efforts like these rise above the level of simple pen pal and provide an opportunity for isolated seniors to be engaged, to feel connected, and to share the tremendous wealth of wisdom they've earned over a long and interesting life.

Citizenship and Political Activism

Many excellent books have been written about the power of youth activism. I highly encourage every young person to stay informed, keeping your eyes, ears, hearts, and minds open to the many complicated, difficult issues facing our country and our world, and to use your energy to fight injustice. There is a long history of political and social activism driven by young people in the United States and around the world. Learn from it, and if you are inspired, get involved. Change doesn't happen on its own. The key to democracy is the power of our collective voices.

KITCHEN TABLE KINDNESS TIP: MAKING YOUR VOICE HEARD

The beauty of sharing your thoughts and opinions with your elected officials is that it can be done from the comfort of your home—all you need is a computer or a telephone. If you are not yet eligible to vote, you may feel that your opinions can't make a difference, but remember that you are among the constituents that politicians have been elected to serve. You have the right to share your concerns and to have them heard. **MAKE TIME** to reach out to your elected officials about issues of concern to you, your family, your peers, or members of your community, especially those who don't have a voice. You can find out how to reach your federal, state, and local elected officials by starting at usa.gov/elected-officials. You can write letters or emails or call to speak to a staff member. If no one is available, leave a message. Remember to be clear about the issue you are addressing, state your concerns briefly, and no matter how upset you are about a problem, always be polite and respectful.

Similarly, you can create and share an online petition to gather signatures in support of an important policy change or in opposition to an injustice you are witnessing. You can explore Change.org (change.org) for existing petitions or create your own.

Participate in a march or rally that has already been organized, or start one on your own with friends and classmates. As you know, social media (discussed in chapter 7) is a great way to learn about or promote an event like this and to generate enthusiasm and encourage participation. Use your **CREATIVITY** in making signs, posters, banners, slogans, T-shirts, hashtags—all of the things that will **RAISE AWARENESS** around the issue.

It is critical to register to vote once you are old enough to do so. Generally, the legal voting age in the United States is 18, but in several states, you may register or preregister at 16 or 17. Search usa.gov for specific information about your state. In the years leading up to your 18th birthday, you can encourage others to vote, **VOLUNTEER** to help members of your community register to vote, and help others make a plan to vote.

Service in School

There are many ways for students to join together to engage in political activism and make an impact on public discourse. Start a diversity and inclusion board if your school does not already have one. Use this platform to give any marginalized individuals or groups a safe place to share experiences and to help brainstorm ways to impact issues of prejudice, exclusion, and discrimination in your school or broader community. It will be important to work constructively and positively with the school administration on this effort. Student groups who feel strongly about injustices can organize sit-ins, petitions, letters to the editor of the school newspaper, and other tools of protest that might spur change. Organize mock debates and schoolwide political discussions during an election year so that students can be informed of different viewpoints. Set up a table at a schoolwide event and share voting information with older students who will be turning 18 in time to vote in an upcoming election. You may even be able to host a voter registration event. The books I've listed below describe these types of efforts and provide insight into the power of young voices and peaceful protest.

Simple Acts is a practical book that focuses on the realistic things you can do in your busy life to become involved in service, citizenship, and political activism. For more inspiration on these topics from a broader perspective, and to learn from those who have blazed a trail in this regard, there are many inspiring books to explore, including:

- *By Any Media Necessary: The New Youth Activism* by Henry Jenkins, Sangita Shresthova, Liana Gamber-Thompson, Neta Kligler-Vilenchik, and Arely M. Zimmerman

- *When We Fight, We Win: Twenty-First-Century Social Movements and the Activists That Are Transforming Our World* by Greg Jobin-Leeds and AgitArte

- *How I Resist: Activism and Hope for a New Generation*, edited by Maureen Johnson

- *Me to We: Finding Meaning in a Material World* by Craig Kielburger and Marc Kielburger

- *The Teen Guide to Global Action: How to Connect with Others (Near & Far) to Create Social Change* by Barbara A. Lewis

- *Road Map for Revolutionaries: Resistance, Activism, and Advocacy for All* by Elisa Camahort Page, Carolyn Gerin, and Jamia Wilson

- *You Are Mighty: A Guide to Changing the World* by Caroline Paul

- *Wake, Rise, Resist: The Progressive Teen's Guide to Fighting Tyrants and A*holes* by Joanna Spathis and Kerri Kennedy

- *Be a Changemaker: How to Start Something That Matters* by Laurie Ann Thompson

The Environment

Greta Thunberg, the young Swedish environmental activist who captured the attention of the world in 2019 by encouraging young people to engage in a climate strike, said, "You are never too small to make a difference." To me this means you are never *too young* or *too busy*. Concern about climate change continues to grow as the impact of global warming on our planet is more clearly understood. Environmental stewardship—care and concern for our planet—is the responsibility of every citizen, but kids and teens feel this movement deeply. While political activism around this issue is important, here I suggest some simple ways that you can make environmental stewardship a part of your daily life by caring for the earth in your own community.

NOTICE when the places where you study, work, eat, and play don't uphold good standards of recycling, trash disposal, and, as appropriate, composting. The use of plastic bags, straws, cups, and utensils is declining, and many companies are exploring ways to cut down on the reliance on single-use plastic products. Learn more about these efforts, support them, and advocate for positive changes in your own community. At a minimum, carry a reusable bag when you go shopping and use a reusable water bottle. **SHARE YOUR IDEAS** with your peers and help to come up with reasonable, affordable solutions.

This may seem obvious, but clean up after yourself, and make the effort to clean up trash that others have carelessly left behind. Littering is rude and selfish. If you can't find a trash can near where you are, take your trash along with you and dispose of it at home or as soon as you find a trash can. As you are moving from place to place during your day, **NOTICE** trash that others have tossed and pick it up. If you see other people littering, try gently reminding them to clean up after themselves. If they refuse to do the right thing, pick up their trash and dispose of it. Be a role model of good behavior in this way. I promise that other kids and adults will notice, and it might make them think about doing the right thing the next time.

If you are planning an outing to the park with friends to picnic, play a sport, or listen to music, consider bringing along a trash bag and some disposable gloves. It may not seem like fun, and it may also take a little bit of preparation, but if you and your friends spend just five minutes working together to clean up the green space where you will be hanging out, it will make a huge difference and set an excellent example for others.

Plant something—a tree, flowers, vegetables, grass, anything that grows and beautifies the green spaces in your community. Planting a tree sapling is a great idea any time, but it is especially meaningful on a number of occasions: around Arbor Day or Earth Day (both in April); in celebration of a milestone in your own life, like a special birthday, sweet 16, or quinceañera; at a religious rite of passage (bar/bat mitzvah or confirmation); or when rejoicing at a new addition to your family or grieving the loss of a beloved relative. If you live in an urban area and don't have an opportunity to plant a tree, there are organizations that will plant trees in public spaces in the United States and around the world. You can find more information on the following websites:

- A Living Tribute (alivingtribute.org)
- Arbor Day Foundation (arborday.org/trees)
- EARTHDAY.ORG (earthday.org)
- Jewish National Fund (usa.jnf.org/jnf-tree-planting-center)
- National Forest Foundation (nationalforests.org)
- One Tree Planted (onetreeplanted.org)

If you are lucky enough to live near one of America's national parks or designated wilderness areas and you enjoy the outdoors, there are many ways to **MAKE TIME TO VOLUNTEER,** helping to keep these national treasures clean and accessible. Explore the National Park Service volunteer program website for more information (nps .gov/getinvolved/volunteer.htm).

RESEARCH established organizations that are making an impact on environmental issues, like the availability of clean water, defor-estation, endangered species, threats to ocean life, climate change, and pollution. Some of the nonprofits working with integrity in these areas include:

- Charity: Water (charitywater.org)
- Clean Water Fund (cleanwaterfund.org)
- Earthjustice (earthjustice.org)

- Environmental Working Group (ewg.org)
- Friends of the Earth International (foei.org)
- Greenpeace (greenpeace.org)
- NRDC (Natural Resources Defense Council; nrdc.org)
- Ocean Conservancy (oceanconservancy.org)
- Rainforest Alliance (rainforest-alliance.org)
- Sierra Club (sierraclub.org)
- WaterAid (wateraid.org)
- Water.org (water.org)

Service in School

If your school doesn't already have one, create an environmental club that can provide information and education about recycling, advocate for composting in the school cafeteria, and place recycling bins in all classrooms and at school events. As mentioned above, there are small changes that can be made—like removing plastic straws from the cafeteria—that can make a meaningful impact. Your club can maybe plant a garden and create events around Earth Day and Arbor Day and organize after-school or weekend park-cleanup events.

Health

A healthy body and mind are two things—when you have them—that many people, especially young people, take for granted. Yet people with illness or disease can have their whole life disrupted and experience tremendous stress and financial hardship. Luckily, a considerable amount of charitable giving and service work is focused on disease-specific causes, **RAISING AWARENESS AND FUNDS** to help people who are suffering, to support their families and caregivers, and to fund research to find cures. Every one of us has been touched by illness, either through our own diagnosis or the experience of a loved one. If this an issue that speaks to you, there are many ways you can help people dealing with challenges around their health.

MAKE TIME TO VOLUNTEER at your local hospital. Years ago, teen volunteers were called "candy stripers" because the red-and-white-striped uniforms they often wore looked like candy. Volunteering in healthcare facilities has evolved, and youth volunteers may be asked to work in administrative offices, the gift shop, directly with patients, or in waiting rooms supporting anxious family members. If you have interest in a healthcare profession, or you just enjoy working with people, volunteering in a hospital setting may be a meaningful activity. Youth volunteers are usually asked to wear a uniform, are given training, and are asked to commit to specific hours on an ongoing basis. Check the website of your local general or children's hospital to find out the age requirements for youth volunteers, the application process, and time commitment. Your parent, guardian, or caregiver will likely need to sign a release form on your behalf.

KITCHEN TABLE KINDNESS TIP: ARTS AND CRAFTS FOR CHILDREN IN NEED

Due to health, privacy, and safety concerns, it is often difficult to volunteer directly with children who are ill or receiving medical treatment. However, there are many ways to brighten the lives of these kids and their families and to show them that someone cares by **SHARING YOUR CREATIVITY**. Below, you'll find a series of kitchen table kindness activities to help children dealing with difficult diagnoses. Invite crafty friends to join you in all of these creative efforts. You may even consider doing some of these projects as part of a birthday or other milestone celebration (learn more about this idea in chapter 3).

⋄ Create colorful cards and letters of encouragement for hospitalized kids. Check out the website for Cards for Hospitalized Kids (cardsforhospitalizedkids.com), an organization that spreads hope and joy to hospitalized children through uplifting handmade cards. There are some simple guidelines to follow, and once you have a stack of cards to donate, you can mail them to the organization, which will distribute them to hospitals and Ronald McDonald House locations across the country.

⋄ With a little bit of fleece and some sharp scissors, you can create no-sew fleece blankets for sick children to use as comforting "lovies." Directions for this easy project can be found on the Doing Good Together website (doinggoodtogether.org/bhf /make-no-sew-blankets). Blankets can be donated to a local hospital or foster care agency, or you can connect with Project Linus (projectlinus.org) to donate them to a local chapter. Project Linus is a national nonprofit that has provided handmade blankets to over seven million children since 1995.

- Children who are experiencing a difficult illness typically spend long, boring days (sometimes weeks or months) in the hospital. You can ease the boredom and spread some joy by creating activity kits for them, like beads and string for friendship bracelets or packets of coloring pages and crayons.

- Sew, iron, or glue patches onto superhero capes, and donate them to your local children's hospital. Simple child-sized capes can be cut out of bright fabric or felt, and you can purchase star, heart, thunderbolt, or other design appliqués at a craft store. You can also draw shapes with fabric paint or markers.

Service in School

First and most importantly: Take care of your own health, and encourage your friends to do the same. Wash your hands; avoid smoking, vaping, drug use, and alcohol use; visit a doctor regularly; and be sure to get your vaccinations. If you are healthy and well, you will be more productive, successful, and physically able to help others who are not as fortunate.

To that end, organize classmates in your school to host **FUNDRAISERS** for organizations fighting specific diseases or supporting a person who is ill in your school or community. As discussed in chapter 4, many nonprofits host events and maintain websites that make it easy for you to get involved. You and your classmates (or the entire school community) can create a team and participate in a walkathon or road race and ask supporters to contribute to your fundraising page.

Animal Rights

Many young people are animal lovers, and many feel a particular attachment to the dogs, cats, and other pets that are beloved members of their own families, as well as the animals that live in the wild. Sadly, abandonment, mistreatment, and cruelty to animals are common. If you care about the welfare of domestic animals, there are many ways you can volunteer in your community to help those that have been mistreated or are in need of loving homes. In some areas, you may be able to volunteer with wildlife rescue organizations that work to find, rescue, and rehabilitate orphaned and injured wild animals.

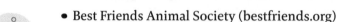

RESEARCH national organizations to identify local shelters or humane societies where you can **MAKE TIME TO VOLUNTEER** working with animals.

- ARF (arflife.org)
- ASPCA (aspca.org)
- Best Friends Animal Society (bestfriends.org)
- The Humane Society of the United States (humanesociety.org)
- Maddie's Fund (maddiesfund.org)

The volunteer work you will be asked to do at an animal shelter may not be glamorous (cleaning out cages, washing blankets, feeding or walking the animals, or simply petting them), but the time you spend will certainly be appreciated by the animals and the shelter staff.

You can search the Humane Society's database of wildlife rescue and rehabilitator locations (humanesociety.org/resources /how-find-wildlife-rehabilitator) to find an organization where you can **VOLUNTEER** with wildlife or **LEARN** how to assist injured animals you might encounter. You can also serve as an advocate, **RAISING AWARENESS** about the appropriate treatment of animals in their natural habitats (not to feed them human food or take them as pets, etc.).

If you are not able to volunteer directly with them, there are other ways you can support animals in your community and around the world.

- **COLLECT** canned food, treats, and pet toys for donation to the shelter or humane society.
- **NOTICE** when a homebound, ill, or elderly neighbor is having difficulty caring for their pet, and offer to help.

- If a neighbor or friend will be hospitalized or traveling, offer to care for their pets while they are away.

- Start a **FUNDRAISER** for the World Wildlife Fund (worldwild life.org), the National Audubon Society (audubon.org), or the Humane Society (humanesociety.org). This is a fun activity around Earth Day in the spring or as part of your Service in School efforts (see below).

KITCHEN TABLE KINDNESS TIP:
CHEW TOYS AND BLANKETS

With a few simple tools—some scraps of fabric or fleece, an old tennis ball, or an empty plastic water bottle—you can **SHARE YOUR CREATIVITY** and create dog chew toys or small blankets for shelter animals. Easy DIY instructions can be found online. An added bonus: these projects are sustainable and reuse items that might otherwise be discarded.

Service in School

If you feel strongly about fighting cruelty against animals, educate yourself on puppy mills, hunting, and the use of animals in the clothing industry or in scientific research. Identify a venue for sharing this information with your classmates. You can create a club that supports the mission of the ASPCA or PETA and host a **FUNDRAISER** on behalf of a local animal rescue shelter. As mentioned above, you can also share your concern for wild and endangered animals with your classmates as part of your green or environmental club efforts and host an awareness campaign or fundraiser around Earth Day or World Wildlife Day (proclaimed by the United Nations as March 3 every year). While it may be difficult to bring animals to an academic setting, you can always bring your knowledge and concern for wildlife and encourage others to make ethical choices.

NOW IT'S YOUR TURN

Jot down some notes about the ideas that have been sparked by this chapter. So, what's your *why*?

Ask yourself these questions, then talk them through with a friend or peer group:

- What are my skills, talents, and interests?
- What are my favorite activities?
- What am I really good at?
- Who are the people I can help, and how?
- What are the social justice issues that concern me?
- What other issues am I passionate about?
- What are one or two things I can do—today, this week, this month—to make a difference in these issues?

Don't Count the Hours; Make the Hours Count

Changing the Narrative on Community Service Requirements

Over the past 20 years or so, there has been a movement among educators to create mandatory (required) community service requirements for students. For some schools, this means that each teen must complete a certain number of community service hours during high school in order to graduate. For others, community service hours are given out as "consequences" for breaking rules, which seems counterintuitive and harsh. Serving others, volunteering, and sharing kindness are rewarding activities that should be encouraged and applauded, not made to seem like punishment. Still other schools allow students to intern or volunteer for community organizations to earn class credit. In recent years, there has been a lot of discussion in educational circles around whether community service should be mandatory or simply encouraged and promoted. There is a catchy name for this issue: *"Volunteer vs. Voluntold."*

As you think about service requirements, ask yourself a few questions. Do you think mandatory service is unethical, amounting to forced servitude, as some have suggested? Or does requiring service have the potential to open your eyes and heart to the needs of others so that you feel an emotional connection? If you are required to do something and that activity creates new, fun, and meaningful experiences, is it possible that you might be inspired to continue on your own? If good things come of it, does it even matter whether it was your idea or not? There are arguments on both sides that are worth exploring and understanding, and hopefully this chapter (and this book) will convince you to find ways to help others regardless of whether it is required by your school. I hope you will agree that, at the end of the day, if you helped even one person and felt good about doing it, it was worthwhile.

In this chapter, you'll **LEARN** the difference between community service and service learning and discover more about the inherent value of service in your life for your education, personal growth, and happiness. The chapter also encourages you to **RESEARCH AND NOTICE** the needs of people in your community; gives you the tools to find the right **VOLUNTEER** opportunities to match your interests and skills; and provides some tips to make the time you spend volunteering meaningful and fun.

There Are More Than Two Sides to the Story

There is research that suggests that requiring young people to do community service has many benefits. As Dr. Benjamin Oosterhoff wrote in *Psychology Today*, mandatory community service:

- teaches you how to get involved and make an impact;
- connects you to your community;

- improves civic engagement (see the "Defining Civic Engagement" sidebar); and

- can enhance academic performance.

Certainly, being told that you *must* do some type of volunteer work to fulfill the requirements of being a student in your school will ensure that you make time for community service that you might not otherwise do, given your busy schedule. I hope you'll see throughout *Simple Acts* that the time spent doing this work can also be fun and worthwhile.

In an article for the New York Times, Stewart Ain reported that teens who were surveyed on this issue said that mandatory service opened their eyes to injustices and the needs of others, and that what began as a required activity quickly turned into a voluntary one. They began the work because they had to do it; they continued the work because they wanted to do so. This makes lots of sense. Volunteering may introduce you to an organization you've never heard of that deals with an issue that you care about, and you may be pleasantly surprised to realize that there is something you can do to help. As with anything in life, you need exposure to people, ideas, and experiences to understand and appreciate them. Of course, this requires an open mind and a willingness to show up, listen, learn, and—most importantly—participate.

DEFINING CIVIC ENGAGEMENT

Civic engagement is an overarching phrase that encompasses all of the things we are talking about in this book—volunteerism, supporting our neighbors, caring for our environment, voting—all of which are done in an effort to improve quality of life for everyone in the community. *Merriam-Webster.com* defines *civics* as "a social science dealing with the rights and duties of citizenship." So *civic engagement* means engaging, or participating, in these rights and duties, which include following the rules (laws) in order to keep yourself and others safe and being responsible community members. Above and beyond this baseline, civic engagement involves fulfilling your responsibility to be helpful and respectful to others and to contribute in a way that makes a positive impact.

On the other side of the argument over mandatory community service, students, families, and even some educators have challenged these requirements. Lawsuits have been filed claiming that mandatory service is unethical and unconstitutional and undermines teens' motivation to do it in the first place. Some have gone so far as to say it amounts to involuntary servitude or make the argument that teaching values is the responsibility of parents and guardians and that schools should focus on academics and not attempt to teach morality to students. All of the lawsuits failed, and in fact there are many ways that schools instill values in students every day: by setting expectations and establishing rules around acceptable, respectful, helpful behavior (throwing out trash in the lunchroom, paying attention in class, and treating classmates with kindness, for example). So encouraging or even requiring students to consider the needs of others and to volunteer in the community (particularly if students are given choice in how they do it) is well within the limits of the education system's purpose. What's more, this type of requirement should never be equated with slavery—it is offensive to do so in light of the cruelties and suffering enslaved people faced throughout history and continue to face today. But some educators do make a compelling case against mandatory service, pointing out that you may need to use any available free time you have to earn money to support yourselves or your families or to pay educational expenses; requiring service can distract from your academic goals; andforcing you to volunteer will turn you off of community service before you even have a chance to experience it.

While there is some validity to these arguments, I think they underestimate your ability as a young adult to manage busy schedules and your genuine desire to help others and make a difference in the world. On balance, it is important for all involved to manage expectations, understand limitations (for example, excusing teens who have legitimate reasons they cannot participate), and keep a positive attitude of generosity and kindness. Ultimately, the goal of any service program should be to educate, encourage, and inspire so that you can make your own decisions about where and how to volunteer in ways that make a meaningful impact on your community—and make you feel good in the process.

The Difference Between Volunteering and Service Learning

You may hear various phrases about service and volunteering being used in your school, at a nonprofit organization, on a college tour, or during a job interview. A few definitions may help you **LEARN** and understand the subtle differences between these terms.

Simple Acts is all about *volunteering*. A volunteer is a person who willingly, and without getting paid, gives time, talent, and effort to a cause they care about. A volunteer is someone who helps others out of the goodness of their heart, without any expectation of getting something in return. I hope you'll become a lifelong volunteer—a person who gives joyfully and gains purpose, pride, and satisfaction in doing so.

Service learning is an educational tool that blends studying and volunteering, with a focus on a particular issue or topic. It's part of a school's or class's curriculum, and students do volunteer work as part of their course requirements. Service learning attempts to connect classroom content to community needs. It allows students the opportunity to dive deeper into issues and to reflect on them in a structured way. Many educators believe that providing a service experience to students deepens their understanding of and engagement with people, issues, and the world outside of the classroom. Of course, you have no control over whether your school offers service learning, and some schools simply don't have the resources or time to incorporate these programs into their curriculum. If your school does offer them, I'm sure you'll find that they enhance your learning and may spark your interest in volunteering on your own time.

UNDERSTANDING COMMUNITY SERVICE

You may hear the phrase *community service* when the topic of volunteering comes up. Sometimes this phrase is used as a blanket statement, as in "participating in community service looks good on your college application." Or your school may have a community service club that organizes donation drives, fundraisers, and volunteer events. Typically, though, the phrase *community service* implies that the work is not being done entirely voluntarily. For example, if someone has broken the law, they may be ordered by the court to do community service work as part of their punishment or as a way to repay the community they harmed with their actions. People may also want to do community service to earn hours that are required for a job or school credit, as described above. It all comes down to the idea of intention. Someone who is engaged in community service is not being paid, but they may have a goal, something they are trying (or are required) to achieve in doing the work, so the work isn't driven solely by the "goodness of their heart." Like service learning, however, doing community service may inspire people to volunteer freely later on.

Tips to Get Started on Your Service Journey

According to Dr. Oosterhoff, "Volunteer experiences that provide teenagers with an opportunity to grow, to make friends, to reflect on social problems, and to cultivate a sense of purpose and enjoyment provide them with greater benefits (including greater intention to volunteer in the future) compared to those without these opportunities." Below, I offer some tips for how to cultivate that sense of purpose and enjoyment.

Whether you're trying to find ways to fit volunteering into your busy life because it's a mandatory requirement of your school or because you're simply moved to help out of the goodness of your heart, these tips and resources will help you

- find appropriate and interesting volunteer opportunities;
- keep it social by recruiting and encouraging friends to join you; and
- stay positive and make the most out of the experience.

Finding Volunteer Opportunities

Whether you are looking for a volunteer activity to fulfill service requirements or are simply interested in giving back to the community on your own, there are many local and national organizations that can help you identify appropriate opportunities.

If your school has a service requirement, it may provide guidance on how to complete the hours or point you toward reputable organizations in your community that will accept teen volunteers. Many schools develop relationships with community partners and maintain a list of the types of work available at these organizations, as well as their locations, hours, and contact information. Some schools may even offer community service days with planned events on the weekends or during the week, allowing students to leave classes to volunteer. You should always check with your advisor, your homeroom teacher, or your school's counseling office to see if any of these types of resources are offered.

In order to find volunteer work that speaks to your personal interests and passions, I'd encourage you to go back to the beginning of this book and review chapter 1 and the self-assessment quiz. What are the problems and social justice issues that are most important to you? What makes you angry, sad, worried? Who are the people whose needs touch your heart the most? You should always try to find volunteer work that keeps and holds your interest, as you will be more likely to recruit friends to join you, enjoy your time, and stick with it for the long haul.

A quick online search to **RESEARCH** "volunteer opportunities for teens in [insert your city or state]" may yield several organizations. Your local YMCA/YWCA, Boys & Girls Club, youth recreation league, Jewish Community Center, or houses of worship (church, mosque, temple, etc.) may keep a directory of organizations that welcome youth or family volunteers. If it all seems overwhelming or you don't know where to begin, there are many reputable organizations and websites to explore, some of which allow you to search by zip code for opportunities in your area.

The organizations and websites on the next page offer resources on volunteering, actionable tools you can use to start service projects or clubs, and/or searchable databases to identify volunteer opportunities in your area.

- All Hands and Hearts (allhandsandhearts.org)
- AmeriCorps (americorps.gov)
- Doing Good Together (doinggoodtogether.org)
- DoSomething.org (dosomething.org)
- Family-to-Family (family-to-family.org)
- generationOn (generationon.org)
- Idealist (idealist.org)
- JustServe (justserve.org)
- Points of Light (pointsoflight.org)
- United Way (unitedway.org)
- Volunteers of America (voa.org/find-an-office)
- VolunteerMatch (volunteermatch.org)
- VolunTEEN Nation (volunteennation.org)
- Youth Service America (ysa.org)

The following organizations and websites offer education and resources around philanthropy (charitable giving), compassion, and kindness; tools to help you start kindness clubs; and ways to spread kindness.

- Born This Way Foundation (bornthisway.foundation)
- Channel Kindness (channelkindness.org)
- Charter for Compassion (charterforcompassion.org)
- The Great Kindness Challenge (thegreatkindnesschallenge.com)
- The Joy Team (thejoyteam.org)
- Kindness.org (kindness.org)
- KindnessEvolution (kindnessevolution.org) *Note: This is a database of organizations with a mission to bring more kindness to the world. It's a great one-stop shop.*
- Kindness Matters 365 (kindnessmatters365.org)
- Learning to Give (learningtogive.org)
- SpreadKindness.org (spreadkindness.org)
- World Kindness Movement (theworldkindnessmovement.org)

Keeping It Social (and Fun)

Whether your school requires you to complete service hours or you're inspired to do so on your own, every volunteer outing is more fun with friends. You'll be more motivated to make plans and show up if you know you'll be spending time with people whose company you enjoy. Finding an opportunity for you and your friends to fulfill service hours together will make the burden (if you want to call it that) easier to bear and will make the hours pass more quickly. Ask around among your friends and classmates to find out what issues are most important to them. Narrow down a group of people who share your interests, and ask if they'd like to volunteer with you.

While volunteering together, you'll need to focus, pay attention, be respectful, and get the job done. Every volunteer activity should be approached as important, valuable work (because it is), and you should act as if you are being held to a high standard (because you are). Providing quality work demonstrates respect for the organization and the clients it serves. When you're volunteering with friends—regardless of the nature of the activity—you can hold each other accountable. And once the activity is complete and you've earned your hours, you can celebrate your accomplishment together.

Staying Positive and Getting the Most Out of It

It may seem daunting or stressful to add service work to your busy schedule or even to pause for a moment in your hectic day to do some small act of kindness for a stranger. You may feel spread thin and preoccupied with the many other responsibilities and worries of your busy life. I don't want to add stress or another item to an already lengthy to-do list, one that will only make you resentful or less inclined to do it. But a big part of growing up and becoming an adult is the ability to make good choices. So much in the world is out of our control, but practicing kindness, demonstrating concern for others, and having a positive attitude are all choices we can make. The world is sometimes harsh, and new situations are often difficult to navigate, but if you bring your best self to this work, you are much more likely to be successful and feel a sense of accomplishment and satisfaction.

Remember, doing good makes you *feel* good, and it is always worth your time and effort. If you feel yourself slipping into cynicism or pessimism, here are just a few ways to make volunteering more fun and meaningful.

Recruit friends to share your experience (and make the time pass more quickly). As discussed above, every difficult or boring task—as well as every fun, interesting, or enjoyable experience—is better when you share it with others. Convince friends to join you on a volunteer project, and everyone wins.

Set manageable goals and time limits. The old expression is still true: don't bite off more than you can chew. Every task is easier to accomplish when you break it down into smaller pieces. If you are required or have committed to do 20 hours over a certain period of time, break that down into two-hour segments (if possible). Nonprofits may require you to commit to a minimum number of hours per visit, but they might be flexible with busy teens who are in school and have academic work and other responsibilities. Advocate for yourself and show that you are committed. You want to be sure that you are on-site and working for a reasonable amount of time in order to finish tasks and provide high quality work, but you don't want to stay so long that you get bored, overworked, or stressed about the commitments you might be neglecting elsewhere.

Take a minute to reflect. After your service experience, take some time to reflect. You could do this quietly in your head or through discussion with family or friends. If you enjoy taking notes, writing poetry, or sketching, consider keeping a journal of your volunteer experiences. Even if the time spent was not entirely enjoyable, try to find some moments of meaning and fun and write about them. If you had a great time, reflect on why. Did you meet someone who made you laugh or inspired you to think differently? Did you share a talent that was acknowledged and encouraged? Did you see joy, relief, or gratitude on someone's face that made you realize that one small action from you can have a tremendous impact on someone who is hurting? Did you learn something new about a troubling social justice issue? Are you just bone-tired at the end of the day, but your volunteer experiences helped you **EXPRESS GRATITUDE** for the fact that you have a family, a hot meal, and a bed to return to at home and allowed you to **PAY IT FORWARD**? This type of reflection may feel silly or uncomfortable, but if you give it a chance during a quiet moment on your ride home or while describing your experience to a family member, you may find that it brings more meaning to your volunteer work. If you keep notes, be sure to save them so you can look back on your full experience at the end of the project. You might even find inspiration for a college essay or an interesting story to tell on a job interview some day in the future.

Talk about it. One of the best ways to fully appreciate an event or experience is to tell others about it. The retelling of the story and giving a description of the people, place, and activities can spark a deeper understanding of why the work was important in the first place. Always start with a positive and highlight the good aspects before any complaints. (Side note: This is good advice for most of life! When speaking to a coworker, a friend, or a family member, always say something nice first.) When talking about the difficult or boring parts of your service experience, try to do it in a way that explains why a situation might have gone badly and to think of ways to improve it the next time. In telling others about your story, you are educating them on ways they might want to be involved, showing them how great the experience was for you (and how good it made you feel), and setting a positive example of how to incorporate service into their busy lives. You are spreading the *good* news about service to others.

Everything comes down to attitude and perspective. The glass can either be half-empty or half-full. You can see service work as burdensome, boring, and a waste of time, or you can see it as a challenge, an opportunity, an adventure, and a gift that you are giving to others—and to yourself. The choice is yours, and I hope you'll choose to stay positive.

NOW IT'S YOUR TURN

Jot down some notes about the ideas that have been sparked by this chapter. Taking time to consider your answers will help you move beyond "checking the box" on service hours.

Ask yourself:

◦ Do I understand the service requirements for my school (if there are any)?

◦ How can I fulfill service requirements or my own wish to volunteer in a way that fits into my busy schedule?

◦ What issues are important to me? How can I identify a volunteer activity that uses my strengths and talents to make an impact on that issue?

◦ Can my school help me find that activity, or am I on my own?

◦ Can I commit to continuing the volunteer work even after I have fulfilled any service requirements? If so, how many hours can I devote?

◦ Can I find a friend who wants to volunteer with me? Who might that be?

◦ What can I do to make my service hours more meaningful and fun?

3

Elevate Your Celebration

Honoring Happy Occasions by Giving Back

As you get older, you and your family will likely recognize many milestones that mark important steps along your journey to adulthood. For example, every birthday is an opportunity to appreciate you and the day you were born. Beyond birthdays, there are other special moments when your family and friends might gather to witness, honor, and celebrate you. These events might include a confirmation or First Holy Communion, a quinceañera or sweet 16, a bar or bat mitzvah, an Upanayana or Samavartana, the completion of Qur'anic schooling, school graduation, or moving up to the next grade. All of

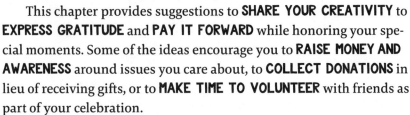

these moments can be honored in a particularly special way by allowing the guest of honor—YOU—to decide how you might like to **PAY IT FORWARD** and share the joy of the occasion with others. You can give back in a small but meaningful way that shows your gratitude for the moment you are experiencing and the support of your family and friends.

When you were a child, if your family was able and inclined to create a celebration for your birthday, there may have been many things that made the day fun: cake, games, friends, decorations, gifts. Now that you are older, you may not need a lot of fanfare and presents to feel loved and appreciated. It's enough to be with people that you love, doing things that you enjoy. You should acknowledge happy, important moments in any way that feels appropriate for you and your family, and I suggest that you can also find space within your celebration to share the joy of your special day with others.

This chapter provides suggestions to **SHARE YOUR CREATIVITY** to **EXPRESS GRATITUDE** and **PAY IT FORWARD** while honoring your special moments. Some of the ideas encourage you to **RAISE MONEY AND AWARENESS** around issues you care about, to **COLLECT DONATIONS** in lieu of receiving gifts, or to **MAKE TIME TO VOLUNTEER** with friends as part of your celebration.

Five Ways to Honor Your Special Moments with Kindness and Generosity

1. Host a Gathering with a Hands-On Service Project

This whole chapter is about inserting some goodness and generosity into your milestone moments, but here I list some simple ideas for creating party with a purpose, a gathering where you invite friends to join you in a hands-on service project. You want your service work to be fun, engaging, and hopefully enlightening for your guests while still allowing time for socializing, eating, music, games, or whatever else you enjoy.

Bake and donate to your local first responders. If you and your friends enjoy being in the kitchen together, consider hosting a gathering where you bake cookies, cupcakes, or other sweet treats. After enjoying some yourselves, package them up on paper plates or in plastic bags and deliver them to your local fire station, EMT station, or hospital emergency room. For an additional fun activity, you can **SHARE YOUR CREATIVITY** and decorate colorful stickers to attach to each bag or write notes of appreciation and encouragement to include in your delivery. As we learned in 2020, and are constantly reminded when natural disasters strike in our communities, first responders risk their lives every day to protect ours. Sharing the sweetness of your celebration with them is a wonderful way to **EXPRESS GRATITUDE** and show support.

Create comfort kits for kids. Over 400,000 children transition in and out of foster care each year in the United States. Frequently, this move happens so quickly that they are forced to carry their belongings in plastic garbage bags. Additionally, 1 in 30 children in the US face homelessness each year. If you are moved to help provide some comfort and dignity to these children, some of whom might be living in your own community, you can rally friends and family to create comfort kits or bags of essentials. This project will require that you **COLLECT** or purchase some new items, as it is important to provide clean, unused items to children who are navigating the foster care system or are experiencing homelessness. You might also be able to request donations of these items from local merchants or the managers of national chain stores in your area. You'll likely be surprised and delighted to see how many retail store owners are willing to donate items to a project supporting kids in need. Reach out to social service agencies serving foster children or people experiencing homelessness in your community before collecting anything to be sure you are donating the most needed items and are following all guidelines. Comfort kits can take many forms, but might include:

- a tote bag or other sturdy reusable bag that the child can keep
- a blanket, stuffed toy, or other comfort item
- a toothbrush and toothpaste and/or other hygiene items
- socks, gloves, or mittens
- a book or a sketchpad with crayons/pencils/markers
- a water bottle

If you are unsure about how to connect with local homeless shelters or social service agencies serving children in foster care, there are several searchable databases online. The National Coalition for the Homeless lists a few directories that allow you to search for homeless shelters in your area (nationalhomeless.org). Some larger cities also have a Department of Homeless Services that can be helpful. Local houses of worship, like churches, temples, and mosques, are also good sources of information, as many maintain homeless shelters within their buildings or work to support those living marginally in the community. To find services helping children in foster care, the US Department of Health and Human Services maintains a database of child welfare information for every state (childwelfare.gov/nfcad). A quick internet search should also provide contact information for local social service agencies.

I encourage you to support children in your own community as described above, but there are several national nonprofits working in this area as well. These organizations suggest a variety of ways to help children in foster care or who are living marginally, and some will help you identify local agencies and shelters that will gladly accept any **FUNDS YOU RAISE** or **DONATIONS YOU COLLECT**. You may also be able to inquire about finding ways to **VOLUNTEER YOUR TIME** supporting the kids.

- Comfort Cases (comfortcases.org)
- Family-to-Family (family-to-family.org)
- Pajama Program (pajamaprogram.org)
- Project Night Night (projectnightnight.org)
- Together We Rise (togetherwerise.org)

KITCHEN TABLE KINDNESS TIP:
NO PARTY? NO PROBLEM!

While this chapter suggests hosting a gathering of friends and family to honor your special moment with service and kindness, all of the **CREATIVE**, artistic, and hands-on activities listed in this chapter can be done at home by yourself or with your immediate family, and they certainly don't need to be done as a part of your birthday or other milestone. Many of these, including the Stars of HOPE project, are also perfect activities for holidays like Thanksgiving or simply for when you have some spare time and want to use your creative energy to help others.

Create art to donate. Drawing and painting are fun and relaxing activities, even if you don't believe you have any artistic talent. Everyone can **CREATE** a drawing of a heart, a rainbow, or a smiley face, and that art might bring a smile or some comfort to someone who is struggling. You and your guests can paint pictures or colorful cards to donate to a local nursing home or senior center, children's hospital, or Ronald McDonald House (rmhc.org).

If you're looking for inspiration, download coloring sheets from the Color a Smile website (colorasmile.org). Over the last 25 years, Color a Smile has collected and distributed over one million drawings to senior citizens, our active-duty military, and hospitalized children. The organization sends art to anyone in need of a smile.

You can also create Stars of HOPE (starsofhopeusa.org) for the New York Says Thank You (NYSTY) Foundation. NYSTY was founded after the terrorist attacks of September 11, 2001, and it gathers volunteers to travel around the United States each summer to help rebuild communities that have been touched by tragedy (a hurricane, tornado, wildfire, etc.). The Stars of HOPE program grew out of this work, as volunteers would decorate wooden stars with positive, hopeful messages and hang them from trees and fences around areas struggling to recover. While the original Stars of HOPE project involved painting wooden stars, the organization recently created a virtual star—a simple coloring sheet—that can be downloaded from the website and printed. The decorated star drawings can be given to first responders, hospital or nursing home staff, and active-duty military or veterans, or they can be displayed around neighborhoods struggling after a natural disaster.

Write letters to isolated seniors. The COVID-19 pandemic highlighted mental health issues like social isolation and depression, particularly among elderly people who were at significant risk of contracting COVID-19. Loneliness among seniors was not a new phenomenon, but it was exacerbated by the quarantine. It became clear that there was an urgent need to reach out to our elderly neighbors and family, in any way possible, to remind them that they were loved and remembered. Sitting together with friends to compose cards and letters to isolated seniors is a wonderful way to reach out and give back. Your local nursing homes, assisted living facilities, and senior centers would gladly accept these messages. You might also want to explore nonprofits like Love for Our Elders, which collects and distributes thousands of letters and videotaped messages to cheer people who are lonely. Love for Our Elders provides detailed advice and instructions for sending handwritten letters on its website (loveforourelders .org/letters). Among other things, the organization requires that letters be handwritten in a large print, avoid religion, and exclude the date. It also encourages writers to be **CREATIVE** with colors and personalization.

CREATE cheerful notes or birthday cards for hospitalized children. Children who are hospitalized and experiencing serious illness are often isolated, sad, and understandably scared. You can spread some sunshine and love to these kids by writing and decorating encouraging cards and letters and deliver-ing them to your local children's hospital, rehabilitation center, or Ronald McDonald House. If you want to personalize your letters, you can also explore the nonprofit organization Cards for Hospitalized Kids (cardsforhos pitalizedkids.com), which offers a database of children who have requested cards and provides help-ful suggestions to make this activ-ity a success, including a checklist for hosting a card-making event. You can also support the Confetti Foundation, which supplies birth-

day party kits to children whose condition forces them to spend their birthday in the hospital. Each box includes a handmade birthday card. Below are some simple instructions provided on the Confetti Foundation's website (confettifoundation.org/make-birthday-cards) that will help you create appropriate cards and letters:

- Keep messages positive and cheerful, and make sure the cards say "Happy Birthday." You can add other messages, but those should be general and not include phrases like "Feel Better" or "Get Well," since you are unaware of the recipient's condition. Keep it simple with sentiments like "Sending you a smile!" or "I hope this card brightens your day." Don't include any religious messages.

- Include your city/state. The Confetti Foundation says, "Our kids love seeing the different places people are thinking of them."
- No glitter, but feel free to use stickers, crayons, or markers.
- You need not spend money on actual greeting cards—you can use folded construction paper.
- Do not include an envelope.

Put together care kits or snack bags for those living marginally. Ask guests to **SHARE THEIR CREATIVITY** by decorating plain brown or white paper lunch bags with markers or stickers. Instruct them to include messages like "Enjoy your snack!" or "Have a nice day!" If you are able, purchase a few snack items in bulk, like individual bags of crackers, chips, cookies, or raisins and small bottles of water or juice. You can also ask for **DONATIONS** from the local supermarket or large discount store or ask guests to bring these items as donations. Create an assembly line, and ask guests to fill each decorated bag with one of each snack item. Coordinate a delivery to a local homeless shelter or homeless street outreach program.

DONATING DECORATIONS

If you and your friends are crafty, consider gathering a small group in advance of your gathering to create colorful decorations that can be repurposed and donated afterward. For example, you can **CREATE** tissue paper-and-pipe cleaner flowers (easy how-to instructions can be found online) and use them as table centerpieces or hang them from the ceiling. After your celebration, you can gather these "flowers" and **DONATE** them to a local nursing home to brighten the dining room or to be distributed to individual residents. Let your creativity and imagination guide you. If you can make something colorful, beautiful, and festive, you can find someone whose day will be brightened by receiving it, and you'll feel so much better than if you simply toss it in the trash.

---

2. Plant Something That Grows

Whether you are planning a celebration or not, you can commemorate a special moment in your life and **PAY IT FORWARD** by planting a tree (or flower, plant, vegetable garden, or shrub—anything that grows and beautifies your surroundings). This small gesture improves the planet and allows you to engage in a conversation with your family and friends about our collective responsibility to care for the earth. It is especially meaningful if your special occasion occurs in the spring or around Earth Day (April 22) or Arbor Day (typically the last Friday in April, but your state may observe it on another day). You can plant a sapling in your own yard or request to plant one in a green space in your town. If you are not able to plant at home or in your community, you can make a small donation to one of the following organizations, which will plant a tree in honor of any occasion:

- A Living Tribute (alivingtribute.org)
- Arbor Day Foundation (shop.arborday.org)
- Earth Day Network's Canopy Project (earthday.org)
- The Jewish National Fund (JNF) (usa.jnf.org)
- The National Forest Foundation (nationalforests.org)
- One Tree Planted (onetreeplanted.org)

3. Host a Fundraiser on or "Donate" Your Special Day

I've devoted a whole chapter in *Simple Acts* (chapter 4) to exploring the ways in which you can have fun while raising money. Sharing the spotlight and joy of your special day by hosting a fundraiser for charity is a really wonderful way of **RAISING MONEY FOR AND AWARENESS** around important causes. It will give you a helper's high to know that the people who want to celebrate you are willing (if they are able) to support an organization that you care about. Generously turning the focus outward with humility shines a light on your values and gives the event special meaning. Some of the fundraising ideas detailed in chapter 4 would be appropriate for, and provide a fun alternative to, a traditional birthday or milestone celebration, so please dive into that chapter for inspiration.

Another option is to officially dedicate and "donate" your special moment to children who aren't able to celebrate theirs. There are a number of different ways to do this and many great organizations that are devoted to this exact mission.

The Birthday Party Project (thebirthdaypartyproject.org) hosts monthly birthday parties for children at homeless and transitional living facilities across the country, and you can "share your birthday" with the children they serve. You can shop its wish list for requested party supplies or gifts for children, **COLLECT** party supplies at your own party, or ask your party guests to bring new toys to donate to the Birthday Party Project in lieu of giving you gifts. After your celebration, contact the Birthday Party Project to learn more about shipping your donations to their headquarters in Dallas, Texas. The Birthday Party Project also encourages people to use the hashtag #ShareYourBirthday on social media platforms when posting about birthday celebration efforts they're having on the organization's behalf.

Create a "birthday party in a box" for a local social service agency, which is both a collection opportunity and a fun activity:

- Ask guests to **DONATE** one item to create a birthday party in a box. Items can include a box of cake mix, a can of frosting, birthday candles, a children's book, and a small inexpensive toy.

- Guests decorate or wrap shoeboxes (top and bottom separately so that they can be opened) and sort the donations into the boxes.

- Guests can also **CREATE** colorful, encouraging birthday cards to include in each box.

One Simple Wish (onesimplewish.org) is an organization that empowers you to spread hope and joy to an individual child in the foster care system or impacted by abuse or neglect. The website allows you to search wishes by category, price range, gender, age range, and location. You can fulfill that wish in honor of your own milestone.

Pencils of Promise (pencilsofpromise.org) is working to make education accessible to underserved children around the world. You can pledge your birthday to fundraise for Pencils of Promise, and the website will provide a campaign tool kit and social media images, photographs, and hashtags that can be used for invitations or distributed at the party.

4. Gather a Group of Friends to **VOLUNTEER** in the Community

To celebrate your special day, you could invite friends to dinner and a movie or some other entertainment, and you might also consider gathering a group to do some good work in your community. Here are a few ideas for a group volunteer outing:

- Clean up a local park, playground, or beach.
- Deliver meals through your local Meals on Wheels program.
- Prepare and serve a meal at a community kitchen.
- Throw a birthday party for children in a homeless or domestic violence shelter.
- Host bingo, a talent show, or a sing-along at a senior center.
- Beautify a green space, with permission (rake, mulch, plant flowers, paint a mural).
- Register as a team for a walkathon.
- Stock shelves or work on the packing and distribution line at a food pantry.
- Volunteer at a school. On a weekend or school holiday, you can paint the fence that surrounds a school or design and paint a mural in the recess yard.
- If you are old enough, participate in a home-building event through an organization like Habitat for Humanity (habitat.org) or Youth Rebuilding New Orleans (yrno.com).

5. Ask for Donations in Lieu of Gifts

Receiving gifts is fun, but as you get older, you may realize you don't need much and would prefer to honor your special occasion by giving to others. Instead of accepting gifts, consider **FUNDRAISING** by asking family and friends to donate to a charity that you have selected. If you are uncomfortable asking for money, you can request **DONATIONS** of specific items. Some examples include:

Canned food: Request donations of canned goods or nonperishable items for your local food pantry. Guests need not spend money on groceries—they likely have a can of soup or box of pasta in their own cabinet to spare. Be sure to check with your local food pantry first to find out exactly what types of items are needed/accepted. If you don't know the location of a nearby food pantry, you can search your zip code on one of the following websites:

- Ample Harvest (ampleharvest.org/find-pantry)
- Feeding America (feedingamerica.org/find-your-local-foodbank)
- Food Pantries (foodpantries.org)

You might also want to place a giving box on a side table at the party. Ask for spare change donations to No Kid Hungry (nokidhun gry.org), which works to alleviate hunger for the more than 13 million US children who live in food-insecure homes. Be sure to include a sign explaining the mission of No Kid Hungry and its impact on childhood hunger in the United States.

Books: If you are a reader, collecting and donating gently used books is a powerful and personal way to give back to younger kids in your community. You will be sharing your love of books with children who may not have many books in their classrooms or at home. Many non-profits and underresourced public-school classrooms and libraries are in need of children's books and would welcome donations. Reach out to local social service agencies, homeless and domestic violence shelters, children's hospitals, Ronald McDonald Houses, literacy programs, foster care agencies, and your local or state Department of Education or **RESEARCH** organizations through resources like the American Library Association. If you'd like to support national and international organizations that collect book donations, explore these websites:

- Better World Books (betterworldbooks.com)
- Books for Africa (booksforafrica.org)
- Donation Town (donationtown.org)
- Promising Pages (promising-pages.org)

Gently used clothing, outerwear, and shoes: Individuals and families who are experiencing homelessness or living marginally lack the disposable income to purchase clothing, shoes, and warm outerwear. A clothing, coat, or shoe **COLLECTION DRIVE** is a great way to encourage folks to donate gently used items that have been outgrown or replaced. You can coordinate this type of collection with your local homeless shelter or homeless outreach organization, or you can arrange to donate everything collected to a local Goodwill Donation Center (good will.org).

Shoes—and specifically sneakers—are a particular passion for many teens. Tap into this by hosting a shoe collection drive for one of the many excellent organizations that are dedicated to providing shoes to people who need them. GotSneakers (gotsneakers .com) is a sneaker-recycling organization that provides all of the tools and resources you need to host a successful shoe drive. Soles4Souls (soles4souls.org) is a nonprofit with the mission of turning gently used shoes and clothing into opportunity, creating jobs, and helping people around the world to break the cycle of poverty.

Sports equipment: Many sports require a ball, glove, racket, or other equipment to be played properly, and this equipment can be an expensive luxury for some families. Collecting and donating new or gently used sports equipment is a great way to share your love of sports with others.

- Check with social service agencies that support young people in your area, like the YMCA/YWCA, Big Brothers Big Sisters of America, or Special Olympics, to ask if they accept donations of gently used sports equipment.

- Explore the following national and international websites for more opportunities to support youth sports:

  ◇ Charity Ball (charityball.org)

  ◇ GOALS Haiti (goalshaiti.org)

  ◇ Peace Passers (peacepassers.org)

  ◇ Sports Gift (sportsgift.org)

  ◇ US Soccer Foundation *Passback* (ussoccerfoundation.org/get -involved/passback)

GIVE AND GET

If family or friends insist on giving you a gift, and you are comfortable asking for monetary donations, ECHOage (echoage.com), Share Your Wish (shareyourwish.com), and Kids Can Give Too (kidscangivetoo.com) are websites that offer the best of both worlds: they allow you to **RAISE MONEY** for charity around your birthday or milestone occasion while still receiving something yourself. You can register with one of these websites, select the charity you would like to support (and, in some cases, what percentage of donated funds to share with the charity), and ask guests to make donations in lieu of gifts. The organizations then collect the funds through online donations and split them, sending money both to you and to your selected charity.

NOW IT'S YOUR TURN

Jot down some notes about the ideas that have been sparked by this chapter. So, how will you honor your special moment with purpose and generosity?

Ask yourself:

- What's one charity or cause I want to support through my next birthday or other special milestone moment?

- How can I get my friends and family involved?

- Am I comfortable asking for donations instead of gifts? If so, should I ask for financial donations or collect specific items?

- How will my invitation explain what I'm doing and why?

- How can I make it fun by incorporating a theme or hosting a fundraiser? (See chapter 4 for more fundraising ideas.)

4

Finding the *Fun* in Fundraising

How to Raise Money and Awareness for a Cause You Care About

When you think of the word *fundraiser*, you might recall taking orders for something your club was selling, hosting a lemonade stand with friends, purchasing from a school book catalog, or collecting trash for cash. These activities were likely some of your first experiences with traditional fundraising, and they were designed to be fun and accessible.

While all of these efforts, and others like them, are worthy and uniquely powered by kids, as a young adult you have a deeper awareness of social justice issues and an understanding of the financial resources that are necessary for a nonprofit to make a real impact. Fundraising is hard, but there are ways for you and your friends to engage in this important work that are both fun for you *and* meaningful to the causes you care about.

First, a little reality check about the different kinds of support that people and organizations truly need. Hands-on, direct service is very important and highly encouraged. In fact, the whole purpose of this book is to motivate you to find time for volunteering and acts of kindness in your busy daily life. I believe you will benefit from serving others as much as your community will benefit from your time, talents, and effort. However, there is a truth that can't be ignored: nonprofit organizations need financial resources to survive and thrive. They need money, and typically lots of it, to make the magic happen, to serve the people who rely on them, to do the actual work—and that's where fundraising comes in. If you can understand the true needs of high-impact nonprofit organizations, you will feel compelled to figure out a way to raise desperately needed funds to help them. In this chapter, I provide some tips and creative ideas that will inspire you to find the *fun* in fundraising.

Use these tips and tools to help **PAY IT FORWARD** by **RAISING MONEY AND AWARENESS** for others who are in need. While covering this important aspect of service, this chapter will also inspire you to **RESEARCH AND LEARN** more about issues that you care about, encourage you to **NOTICE** the needs of the people and organizations in your community, and recommend ways to **SHARE YOUR IDEAS AND CREATIVITY** in planning fundraising activities.

Before You Get Started Fundraising

Work collaboratively with the charity you are supporting to be sure it approves of your efforts and to ensure that you are meeting its most pressing needs. Recruit a team of friends to help. Everything is more fun (and easier) with a committed group of volunteers working together. The organizational, team-building, and leadership skills you gain will help you throughout your life. Solicit donations from local vendors (like pizza parlors, donut shops, or other restaurants), stores (like party supply stores or supermarkets), corporations (which might give money to sponsor the event), and service providers (like

DJs, musicians, or transportation providers). Many of the event ideas listed below will be enhanced (and cheaper to execute) if you are able to get the necessary supplies donated.

It's very important to be sure to **get all of the appropriate permissions and permits** you may need from any authority that has agency over your venue, space, or event. You'll save yourself a ton of headaches, and be more successful overall, if you do everything right from the beginning.

Getting Started: The "Ask"

Raising money is hard work, but it helps if you have a positive and resilient attitude, a thick skin, and a healthy dose of humility. Remember one of the most important elements of fundraising: You're not asking for yourself. You're asking for a person, a cause, or a worthy organization that needs the money. And you're doing a really good thing—raising awareness around an issue and asking others to donate, if they can, because you care about it and want to help.

Whenever I'm doing fundraising work or am training other volunteers to do so, I always ask the same question: "What's the worst thing that someone can say when you ask them for a donation?"

The answer, of course, is "No." The worst-case scenario is that the person turns you down. Perhaps it would be worse if the person were rude, offensive, or unkind to you, but those responses are highly unlikely. A person who can't or doesn't want to donate will most likely just say no, usually apologetically, and that is a totally reasonable and understandable response. Regardless of how much you care about the cause and how passionate and compelling you are in your description, the person you are soliciting may not share your views. And even if they do, they simply may not have the resources to make a donation at this time. If you hear a no, your response should always be "Thank you for your time and consideration." Then, you move on to the next potential donor with a smile on your face and try again. I think you'll find, with time and practice, the answer will usually be yes.

Some Fundraising Tips to Keep in Mind

- Smile and make eye contact.
- Be polite and respectful of each person's time.
- Clearly and briefly state what you are asking for and why. This will require you to understand the mission of the organization for which you are fundraising and be able to quickly articulate it. This is sometimes called an "elevator pitch." How would you describe the issue if you only had an elevator ride in which to do so?
- Be passionate and enthusiastic. Show the person that you care and why they should too. Provide a personal anecdote, tell a story, appeal to the hearts of potential donors.
- Consider suggesting a specific amount to be donated. Be thoughtful about this, and try to understand the financial means of the person you are soliciting. Many times when people are asked to donate to a charity, their response is "How much should I give?" or "How much are other people giving?" Try to anticipate these questions and have an answer prepared.
- Be gracious and grateful for donations, and always thank people whether they are able to give or not.

It may seem like I'm simplifying this challenging activity, but I believe that a big-hearted fundraising volunteer will always be successful and should be respected and appreciated. It helps if you can learn the very important skill of letting rejection roll off your back. It's not always easy, but once you get the hang of it, you'll gain courage.

It doesn't matter if you are collecting coins in a jar or asking for credit card donations online; fundraising is hard work, and every dollar that is donated is important and appreciated. Reaching a lofty goal is exciting, but every little bit helps. Even if you only raise one dollar, that's one dollar more than the organization had before you started fundraising for it, and you should feel proud of the effort.

A NOTE ABOUT GOAL-SETTING

Whether it's earning a good grade on a test or hitting some number of free throws without missing, setting a goal is always helpful in keeping yourself motivated. When it comes to fundraising, you may hope to raise as many dollars as you can for a person, organization, or group in need (and that's an admirable goal), but sometimes a goal lends itself well to a specific dollar amount. For example, you might hear about a particular item that is needed in your community, like a new truck for your local firehouse or a new playground swing set to replace the one that is dangerously in disrepair. Or you may be moved to help someone who is urgently in need, like a person whose home was lost to fire or flood or who needs medical care or equipment. In those instances, you will have a good idea of the amount of money you need to raise, and that will become your goal. Tracking your progress and setting a deadline motivates you and allows you to leverage social media to blast out targeted messages to potential donors. You might encourage people to donate with pleas like, "We're only $100 away from our goal! Will you help us get there by tomorrow?" These types of messages get people excited about being part of something important, and they provide donors the satisfaction of knowing that they helped your fundraising effort cross the finish line.

15+ *Fun-raising* Ideas

What follows is a list of 15 tried-and-true (and a few out-of-the-box) ideas for homegrown fundraising events that may appeal to your energy, enthusiasm, and interests. I've also included five ideas (which you will find in sidebars throughout) that represent a "stretch" beyond what might seem achievable. For these suggestions, you may need to recruit more adult help or interface with national or local organizations, some of which I've suggested. I offer these possibilities to raise the bar for those who might be excited to take on a challenge. You know your community best, so you can decide what activities will entice your neighbors and friends and what will make the most logistical and financial sense. Perhaps something suggested in the pages that follow will spark a whole new idea. The sky is truly the limit. If you can dream it up (and figure out the details), you can do it.

1. Bake Sale

Let's begin with the most traditional (and perhaps the most delicious) fundraising idea: the classic bake sale. This is a great effort any time of year, and especially around Valentine's Day, Mother's Day, Halloween, and the December "giving" holidays of Christmas and Hanukkah. You'll need to recruit multiple volunteers to bake and individually wrap items and check in with your school or venue about rules for food safety and allergens. A bake sale can be held during the school day at lunch, in conjunction with a lemonade stand in the summer, on a parade route, at the finish line of a running race or walkathon, during halftime at a game or intermission at a performance— whenever hungry crowds gather.

INSPIRATION: A LEMONADE STAND WITH A TWIST

You might think a lemonade stand is just a fun afternoon activity for little kids, but there's an organization that is working to change that perception. Alex's Lemonade Stand Foundation (alexslemonade.org) is funding impactful research to help cure childhood cancer while raising awareness and supporting patients and their families. It all started with a front yard lemonade stand.

Alexandra "Alex" Scott was born in 1996 and was diagnosed with neuroblastoma, a type of childhood cancer, before her first birthday. When she was just four years old, Alex held her first lemonade stand and raised over $2,000 for childhood cancer research. By the time of her death in 2004, Alex had raised more than $1 million. Alex's family started Alex's Lemonade Stand Foundation (ALSF) to continue her legacy and raise critically needed funds for research into childhood cancers. ALSF offers hands-on volunteer opportunities and fundraising projects like signature lemonade stands, special-occasion fundraisers, and kickball and other sporting events. It even has a fundraising program that allows athletes to turn their sports achievements into research dollars.

---

2. Car Wash

The car wash fundraiser is a staple—and for good reason. It combines being outdoors with friends, cooling off with water, and offering a needed service. This is an inexpensive and relatively easy activity to plan and execute. You need a lot of volunteers; appropriate space (a long driveway, parking lot, etc.); basic supplies like buckets, sponges, and car wash soap; and access to water and hoses. Of course, a sunny weekend day is your best bet for a good turnout and lots of fun. Recruit friends to create colorful signs, and stand on a visible, busy corner to entice customers.

STRETCH IDEA: CUSTOMIZED LOGO MERCHANDISE

The idea of selling T-shirts as part of various fundraising events is included elsewhere on this list, but the creation and sale of T-shirts or sweatshirts personalized with a logo can also be a great fundraising activity on its own. There are many websites, like Custom Ink (customink.com/fundraising), that make this work easy by allowing you to design and sell merchandise with the specific goal of raising money for charity. Customers order directly from the website, which handles printing and shipping, and a portion of proceeds are sent to you at the end of the sales event.

3. Game Night

Organizing an interactive game night is a fun and simple way to bring people together to raise money. Simple, traditional games like bingo, Pictionary, Monopoly, Jenga, and Twister require very few supplies and provide hours of entertainment. Game night can incorporate many different fundraising elements, like ticket sales, team registrations, refreshment sales, and custom team T-shirts, that make it fun and appealing to large groups of all ages. An original trivia night is great way to challenge attendees' knowledge of each other, their school, or their community.

STRETCH IDEA: VIDEO GAME TOURNAMENT
Video gaming is an integral part of many teenagers' daily lives. If
this is true for you, an all-ages video game tournament could be fun
to organize. Entry fees can be charged, and while this event can be
done virtually, a live event held in an auditorium could draw a large
crowd and provide the opportunity to sell T-shirts and refreshments
as well. There is an organization called Fun Funding (funfunding.org)
that uses gaming as a tool to help people fundraise. It builds technology that encourages people to do good in their daily activities
through an online gaming platform. Users can support causes they
care about by achieving different levels and earning prizes provided
by corporate sponsors.

4. Battle of the Bands or Talent Show

These are fun ideas for **SHARING YOUR TALENT AND CREATIVITY** if
you are part of a garage band, play an instrument, or enjoy singing,
dancing, or telling jokes. A talent show is a great way to involve lots
of talented teens from your school or community, all of whom have
lots of fans who will fill an auditorium to support and cheer for them.
It's important to make a talent show a mix of serious musical perfor-
mances and fun, lighthearted entertainment, so encourage participants to put together group numbers and skits.

5. Sports-a-Thon

The "sports-a-thon" is a classic fundraiser for young people, and it's a
great way to fundraise. Participants raise money by walking, running,
bowling, swimming laps, hitting free throws, spinning, and more.
You'll engage lots of participants, who will each solicit individual
donations in the form of pledges (dollars per lap, per free throw, per
bowling pin, etc.) from family and friends.

STRETCH IDEA: DANCE MARATHON
Similar to the sports-a-thon, the dance marathon is a fun event,
although it may require more planning and organization. It can be
pledge-based (donors give X amount per hour danced) or more of
an all-around fundraiser (donors give X amount if dancers complete
some impressively long number of dance hours). You might also

consider selling song dedications, shout-outs to individual dancers, T-shirts, and refreshments. It will be important, as with so many of these events, to try to get items donated by local vendors and suppliers (DJ services, refreshments, etc.), and you'll need to work collaboratively with your school, place of worship, or community center to find a sufficiently large venue. Dance marathons typically last 24 hours but can be shorter or longer depending on the limitations of your space. It's important to provide food and water to the dancers and to build in breaks so that everyone stays healthy and hydrated. Of course, you can make your own rules and create teams so that dancers can tag each other out or take turns over long stretches. The details are up to you, but the most important part is to make the event fun and safe.

6. Community Cleanup / Planting Project

A park cleanup event is great because it serves two purposes: you and your friends will be actively improving a park, green space, beach, or neighborhood, and you'll simultaneously be fundraising for a good cause. This fundraiser requires you to **NOTICE** the green spaces in your community that are in need of cleaning and improvement. You can invite individuals or teams to ask for pledges for the number of bags of trash collected, the amount of time spent working, or the number of bulbs planted. You can incorporate a bake sale or T-shirt sale. This is a great event to hold in honor of Earth Day (April 22nd); Arbor Day (date varies by state); National CleanUp Day (the third Saturday of September); World Environment Day (June 5th); or the Jewish holiday of Tu BiShvat, the "New Year of the Trees," which is celebrated as an ecological awareness day.

7. Dress Down Day

This idea has been around for a long time, but it still works in school settings where a formal dress code is in place. Everyone who wants to participate pays a small fee (it can be as little as $1 or $5) to wear jeans or another typically discouraged item of clothing, like baseball caps or sweatpants, on a specific day, and all of the proceeds are donated to charity. Of course, you will need the full support and cooperation of the school administrators. You can also combine this effort with a gently used clothing **DONATION** drive or a denim recycling program. An organization called Blue Jeans Go Green (bluejeansgo green.org), created by Cotton Incorporated, collects gently used denim at retail stores and recycles it back to natural fibers so it can be transformed into something new.

8. Movie Night

An old-fashioned movie night can incorporate lots of fundraising elements, such as ticket sales, refreshments, a bake sale, or a costume contest related to the theme of the movie.

9. Fashion Show

If your artistic talents are directed toward fashion—whether you're interested in designing, sewing, or knitting clothing; painting or drawing on shoes or denim; or making other types of wearable art—you can **SHARE YOUR CREATIVITY** by hosting a fashion show and inviting other teen designers to participate. You might also consider hosting a reality show–style challenge competition and fashion show where participants are asked to create clothing out of items like paper, plants, or recycled plastics. Inviting teens of all shapes, sizes, and abilities to serve as models and asking visual artists to decorate the runway or photograph the event  are great ways to be inclusive and engage a large group of people who want to share their talents.

STRETCH IDEA: SHAVE HEADS IN SOLIDARITY WITH CHILDHOOD CANCER SURVIVORS

St. Baldrick's Foundation (stbaldricks.org) is a volunteer-powered charity committed to supporting research to find cures for childhood cancers. The primary fundraising activity of St. Baldrick's is hair-shaving events, which are interactive and fun and demonstrate support for children who have lost their hair due to chemotherapy.

---

10. Dog Walking / Dog Party / Pet Grooming

Any activity that appeals to animal lovers (as donors, volunteers, or participants) is going to be a success. You and a group of friends can offer dog-walking services or organize an outdoor "dog party" at a local dog park, where you can charge admission fees and sell refreshments and T-shirts. This is a great way to fundraise for the ASPCA or an animal rescue shelter in your area. While offering full grooming services is difficult (don't try to cut the hair or nails of an animal if you have no experience doing so or without proper training), you can still offer pet washing and pet-safe "styling" services with very little or no overhead costs.

11. Gift Wrapping

One of the key aspects of a successful fundraising event is offering a service that people are willing to pay for (in the form of donations). Everyone loves giving gifts, but very few people love wrapping them, so consider **MAKING TIME TO VOLUNTEER** with a gift-wrapping service. Especially around the holidays, when people are overwhelmed with many tasks on their to-do lists, a gift-wrapping service might attract many excited and generous customers/donors. You can reach out to an independently owned department store or toy store to ask about hosting a gift-wrapping fundraiser around the holidays, and you may be able to set up a table at the local mall as long as you receive permission to do so. This is also an activity that can be done at school on a weekend, at a house of worship, or at another venue if you promote the event well in advance so people will bring the gifts they've previously purchased to be wrapped.

12. Craft Sale

The December and January "giving" holidays of Christmas, Hanukkah, Kwanzaa, and Three Kings Day are typically filled with gift giving and decorating, and many people enjoy the thoughtfulness of handcrafted items. **CREATIVE AND CRAFTY** teens can make things like Christmas tree ornaments or beeswax Hanukkah candles to sell around the holidays. Setting up a table to sell your crafts at a larger craft fair is probably the easiest way to do this, but you may be able to find a local retail store to carry your items or ask your school if you can set up a table in the lobby during holiday concerts and pageants.

STRETCH IDEA: TEEN COOKBOOK

A custom cookbook is a favorite fundraiser for many school parent associations and faith groups, and if you and your peers enjoy cooking, you might consider publishing one of your own. There are many cookbook-publication websites that allow contributors to upload their favorite recipes and that will handle all of the formatting, graphic design, and distribution details. A few examples include CreateMyCookbook (createmycookbook.com) and Morris Press Cookbooks (morriscookbooks.com).

13. Candy-Grams, Secret Santa Messages, Valentines, or Flowers

I originally saw this idea used during intermission at a community theater production in which my daughter was performing. In addition to a very robust bake sale, organizers were selling "candy-grams" for members of the cast. For the donation of a dollar, you could write a note of congratulations or support to a friend or family member performing in the show, and volunteers would attach it to a lollipop and deliver it to that person backstage. This can be done as a Secret Santa or Secret Valentine effort as well, and you can use a wide variety of candies. If you're interested in selling flowers to raise money, the key is to offer the flowers at a time when people want them (Valentine's Day, just before Mother's Day, during prom season, etc.). It's also a great idea to solicit donations from a local florist or nursery.

14. Balloon Bust

Typically, a balloon bust activity goes along with a raffle being held at a larger event. Descriptions of donated raffle items are written on small slips of paper and placed inside balloons, which are then inflated. People purchase balloons and pop them to find out what they've won. You can have different tiers, with each tier representing more or less valuable raffle prizes, and price the balloons accordingly. It's a noisy but fun activity that adds a twist to a traditional "pulling a name out of a hat" raffle.

15. Raffle

Raffles are a great way to raise money. Make no mistake, though: putting together a good raffle is a fair amount of work. You need to check your local legal requirements, solicit and collect raffle items, acknowledge and thank your donors, set the right prices for the raffle tickets, and sell enough tickets to make all of the time and effort worthwhile. There are other types of raffles that don't require donated items, though. A "50/50" raffle is typically used in larger fundraising events, but it is simple and effective. You sell 50/50 raffle tickets over the course of the event or a period of time, then pull one name out of a hat at the end. The winner takes 50 percent of the total amount collected, and the charity takes the other half. You need to set a sufficient price for entry and be aware of your crowd. Can folks afford a slightly higher entry fee? If so, you'll raise more money. If you'd rather be sure that everyone can participate, set the amount lower and try to get everyone to buy a ticket. You'll still raise plenty of money, and the winner will be thrilled with their share no matter what. Other ideas include raffling off being "Principal for a Day" or a prime parking spot at your school or front-row seat at the school musical, band concert, or sporting event. You will need to use your imagination and creativity to collect items or experiences that would appeal to your community.

KITCHEN TABLE KINDNESS TIP:
ONLINE CROWDFUNDING

You have the ability to spread information broadly and quickly, reaching hundreds, if not thousands, of people with one social media post or well-worded email—all from the comfort and safety of home. You can use online crowdfunding tools to fundraise for important causes. Websites like GoFundMe (gofundme.com) and Indiegogo (indiegogo.com) have been designed for ease of use and maximum fundraising capability. The power of social media to amplify important causes and spread positive messages is explored more fully in chapter 7.

Jumping on a Bandwagon: Walks, Runs, and Cycling Events

It's very likely that a cause you care about is already being championed by an organization that is hosting fundraisers. A good way to ease into fundraising is to rally family and friends and sign up for one of these campaigns. Some of the larger, more established campaigns are listed below, but you should search online for organizations that are already working on an issue that concerns you. You may find that an organization is hosting an event in your area and would welcome your participation and personal fundraising efforts. Listed below are some of the notable charitable walks, runs, and cycling events that occur throughout the year in communities across the United States and around the world.

Walkathons/Road Races/Fun Runs

- AIDS Walk
- Buddy Walk (National Down Syndrome Society)
- Girls on the Run (building confidence and health in girls)
- Heart Walk (American Heart Association)
- JDRF One Walk (Junior Diabetes Research Foundation)
- Light the Night Walk (Leukemia & Lymphoma Society)
- Livestrong Challenge Fun Run/Walk (Supporting Livestrong's programs for people affected by cancer)
- Making Strides Against Breast Cancer (American Cancer Society)
- Out of the Darkness Walk (American Foundation for Suicide Prevention)
- Relay for Life (American Cancer Society)
- Step Out Walk to Stop Diabetes (American Diabetes Association)
- St. Jude fitness and sports fundraisers, including St. Jude Walk/ Run and the St. Jude Heroes Program (St. Jude Children's Research Hospital)
- Susan G. Komen Race for the Cure (funding breast cancer research and support for women with breast cancer)
- Walk MS (National Multiple Sclerosis Society)
- Walk to End Alzheimer's (Alzheimer's Association)
- Wounded Warrior Project Carry Forward 5K (supporting soldiers gravely injured while serving in the military)

Cycling Events (Indoor and Outdoor)

- AIDS/LifeCycle

- Bike MS (National Multiple Sclerosis Society)

- Cycle for Survival (Memorial Sloan Kettering Cancer Center research of rare cancers)

- The St. Jude Ride (St. Jude Children's Research Hospital)

Some Final Words of Advice and Inspiration

- Work with peers to come up with a unique fundraising campaign (everything is more fun with friends).

- Be detail-oriented and create a checklist of everything you will need to collect, create, and do to make the effort successful.

- Ask for help and donations from the community—individuals, retail stores, and vendors.

- Set a realistic but ambitious goal and timeline.

- Craft a passionate and compelling pitch for your fundraising effort. Remember to make it personal and tug on heartstrings. It's not manipulative—your pitch is honest and genuine, and you're raising money for a good, and often emotionally charged, cause!

- Use the power of social media to amplify your message.

- Thank your donors, sponsors, and volunteers—repeatedly and publicly.

- At the end of your event or campaign, review what worked and what didn't.

- Feel proud of every dollar you raised, because no matter how much money you will be donating to the charity you are supporting, it will be gratefully accepted and appreciated.

NOW IT'S YOUR TURN

Jot down some notes about the ideas that have been sparked by this chapter. How can you have fun while fundraising for a cause you care about?

Ask yourself:

◦ What or whom would you like to support with your fundraising activity?

◦ What are two or three creative fundraising activities you would enjoy planning?

◦ What activity do you think would be the most interesting and appealing to your friends and community members?

◦ What is your ambitious but realistic goal?

◦ How will you thank your donors?

◦ How will you celebrate your accomplishments (whether you reach your goal or not)?

5

Doing Well by Doing Good
Understanding Social Entrepreneurship

You may have heard the phrase *Doing well by doing good* and wondered exactly what it means. It perfectly captures the concept of social entrepreneurship, which we'll discuss in this chapter. Social entrepreneurship has grown in popularity over the last several decades, as innovative people have harnessed their concern for social justice issues into the creation of a business (or "social enterprise") that makes a positive impact. Many bright, caring people have figured out how to sell products and services that **RAISE FUNDS AND AWARENESS** to help solve a social problem while also making money for themselves.

Research suggests that this trend is growing in popularity. Young people today are just as concerned with making a positive impact on the world as they are with making money. A 2017 Gallup poll found that 40 percent of Gen Z students in grades 5 through 12 plan to start their own business. There are many reasons young people may want to do this. For example, a Nielsen study cited by *Forbes* found that two of the key factors driving young people to be entrepreneurs are "the planet" and living "a purposeful life." Of course, this do-good mentality is combined with the very necessary and understandable desire to be successful, to avoid starting adult life with a mountain of debt, and to achieve financial independence.

In this chapter, you'll **LEARN** a little about social entrepreneurship as a concept, and if you want to learn more, I've included a list of suggested books that offer instructions and advice for starting your own social venture and books about several famous entrepreneurs who have created popular brands that make an impact on social justice issues. You'll also be able to think about ways to **SHARE YOUR CONCERNS AND CREATIVITY** through the business ideas you hatch. If you are successful in launching a social enterprise, you'll be **RAISING MONEY AND AWARENESS** around an important cause.

It may seem overwhelming to even consider creating a social venture of any kind right now. Again, the goal of this book is to help you—a very busy teenager—find time to give back and perform acts of kindness in your already packed schedule. I include all of this information here not to overwhelm you but to challenge you to explore a concept that is bold, exciting, potentially challenging, and certainly time-consuming, but ultimately very rewarding. It may not be something you can even consider at this point in your life, or you may have no interest in ever starting a business from scratch, which is totally fine. The purpose of this discussion is to help you understand social entrepreneurship as a model for social change while perhaps inspiring you to learn more. You never know how you might apply what you've learned to things you will do in the future or how understanding this concept might influence the products you buy or the causes you support later in your life.

Luckily, there are lots of really smart people in business, in the nonprofit world, and on university campuses across the country who study entrepreneurship and have shared step-by-step guidance in a number of books (some of which are listed in this chapter) and other platforms. One of the best things about innovative people is that they typically thrive on connecting and sharing ideas with other smart, creative people, recognizing that this helps everyone succeed. Entrepreneurs tend to live by the motto "We rise by lifting others."

Shopping with Purpose

Sustainable food advocate Anna Lappé said, "Every time you spend money, you are casting a vote for the kind of world you want." The money you spend on a variety of things—clothing, food, shoes, accessories—has the power to make a positive impact on the world. It's important to understand where and how merchandise is made so that you can be sure that the things you buy are not made in sweatshops or by children or enslaved adults. As much as possible, you should support businesses that pay a fair wage to workers and/or engage in fair trade practices, which means that companies in developed countries like the United States pay fair prices to the producers of products in developing countries. To take this idea a step further, you may want to **RESEARCH** and support companies with a mission to give back. These companies may participate in a "buy one give one" program, or they may donate a portion of profits to worthwhile causes. Some popular examples of "buy one give one" companies include these:

- Bombas, which gives away socks to people experiencing homelessness
- STATE Bags, which donates full backpacks to children in need
- This Saves Lives, which donates a packet of nutrition to a child experiencing extreme malnutrition for every snack item purchased
- Warby Parker, which gives away a pair of eyeglasses for each one purchased

Popular companies and products that give a portion of profits to charity include:

- Charity: Water (brand partnerships)
- Ethos water (at Starbucks)
- FEED (bags)

- Lush (bath and body products)
- Newman's Own (grocery items)
- Patagonia (clothing)
- Pura Vida (bracelets)

The Basics of Social Entrepreneurship

Much of the information I share in this section is from the wealth of knowledge and experience that's been collected at the Wharton School at the University of Pennsylvania. In 2001, Wharton established the Wharton Social Entrepreneurship Program, and two Wharton professors, Ian C. MacMillan and James D. Thompson, wrote a book called *The Social Entrepreneur's Playbook*, which is filled with academically tested and real-world-proven advice.

MacMillan and Thompson explain that social ventures are challenging to create and sustain and that making money from them is often difficult. After years of field experience, they believe that it is possible to launch a successful social enterprise that makes some (but not excessive) profits by taking "small steps, focusing on discovery versus outcomes, and being constantly vigilant for the unexpected" (MacMillan and Thompson, 2013, xiii). In other words, you have to hold back from going too fast, listen and learn, and be prepared to pivot when you hit a roadblock. Regardless of whether your idea becomes a reality or is a success long-term, making an effort to start a social venture can provide tremendous skills that you will use throughout your life.

The Social Entrepreneur's Playbook is broken down into three phases, and it walks you through the nuts and bolts of each one. While the book provides a high-level analysis aimed at adults, the basic concepts can be distilled down to make sense for anyone who is launching a new venture, whether it's a neighborhood lemonade stand or a global clothing business, a collection drive for a local food pantry or a large-scale meal delivery program fighting hunger and food insecurity.

Phase One: Pressure Test Your Start-Up Idea.
If you have a great idea, the first thing you'll need to do is research, ask good questions, and listen in order to move from the spark of an idea to a plausible plan. You'll find a great exercise to facilitate the process, called "The 5 Whys," a little later in this chapter.

Phase Two: Plan Your Social Enterprise.
As the saying goes, the devil is in the details, and the more detailed your plan, the more likely it will be a success. See the Creating a Business Plan sidebar for more details on the basic elements of a business plan for a social enterprise.

Phase Three: Launch and Scale Your Social Enterprise.
Taking the leap from a plan on paper to an actual entity is a big deal, and once your social enterprise is up and running, figuring out how to measure, evaluate, and expand it is probably the hardest—and most important—part.

CREATING A BUSINESS PLAN

Later in this chapter, you'll see a few online resources where you can find templates, instructions, and guidance on creating a business plan and launching a social enterprise, but for now, you should understand that having a great idea and a big heart are not enough—you need to have a detailed plan. Business plans can take many forms, but generally, they consist of a few basic elements:

- A Summary: What do you want to do? What problem are you trying to solve?

- A Mission or Vision statement: This is your big, impactful goal, written out in a few words.

- A Market Analysis: Do people want what you are going to make/ the service you are going to provide?

- A Competitive Analysis: Is anyone else already doing what you are proposing? If so, how will you be different?

- A Description of Products and Services: Exactly what will you be making what service will you be providing?

- A Marketing and Sales Plan: How will you promote and advertise what you are doing?

◇ An Operations Plan: How will you produce the product or fulfill the service you are proposing? (This is the nuts and bolts of the plan.)

◇ An Outline of Your Plans to Evaluate and Assess: How will you measure success?

◇ A Financial Plan: What is all of this going to cost, and how will you pay for it?

Another great resource, *Social Entrepreneurship: From Issue to Viable Plan* by Terri D. Barreiro and Melissa M. Stone, offers a description of how the "spark" of an idea might come to you as a social entrepreneur. Barreiro and Stone write, "An injustice, a social justice issue that is not well addressed, or a cause that has affected them personally often first motivates social entrepreneurs" (2013, 24). This makes sense. If you notice a problem or injustice, whether it affects your community or you personally or is a concern in the wider world, you will be motivated to do something about it. I would go further and say that to motivate social entrepreneurship in you, the issue usually has to speak to something inside of you or affect something or someone you care about. Your heart needs to feel something for your brain to kick into gear.

However, Barreiro and Stone caution about the gap between enthusiasm and a venture's actual successful launch. It's hard to make a meaningful difference in a really difficult problem. Caring about a problem isn't enough: moving from concern to action requires a great deal of courage and resilience. You need to do the work, ask the hard questions, and be an active listener. So, to start a social enterprise, you have to care deeply, muster the courage, and then develop the leadership skills to make it happen. That might seem really daunting. But there are resources, tools, and successful people—probably many in your own community—who have navigated this challenging territory before. You should take advantage of all of these things.

Testing out your idea to see if it is feasible requires you to "build a deeper understanding of [the people who will benefit] and of the community, policy, and competitive environment of the issue" (Barreiro and Stone, 2013, 18). Barreiro and Stone describe a method for moving from concern to action called "The 5 Whys." This brainstorming exercise should be done with a team so you can gather as many different ideas as possible. It looks like this:

1. Write down the problem.

2. Ask **why** the problem happens, and write down all the answers.

3. Ask **why** one or more of those answers is the case, then write down all the answers.

4. Repeat step 3 until the team is in agreement about the problem's root cause(s), asking **why** a total of five times (or more!).

Asking *why* and being thoughtful about the answer seems like a pretty good way get to the bottom of any problem. Barreiro and Stone go through an excellent example (from a school system in Minnesota) that demonstrates how your first reaction to a problem may not be exactly right and why you may need to dig a little deeper.

1. Why are third graders missing days of school? Answer: they miss the bus.

2. Why do kids miss the bus? Answers: they don't wake up on time; their parent/caregiver leaves for work before they leave for the bus; they don't have warm clothes to wear at the bus stop; they are sick.

3. Why don't they have warm clothes? Answers: their parents have poverty-level incomes; they are new refugees (from a warmer climate) and didn't anticipate needing cold-weather clothing.

4. Why don't we provide warm clothes to new arriving refugees? Answer: refugee service organizations don't have enough donated clothes to give or the funds to purchase such expensive items.

5. Why don't people in Minnesota donate extra winter coats that their children have outgrown? Answer: there is no concerted effort to get these items donated, no easy way to donate, and no system to collect and distribute them.

The conclusion of this exercise led to the creation of a coat donation campaign to benefit new refugees and others who needed warm coats. "The need for warm coats" probably wouldn't have been the first answer to the original question, but after a lot of digging and thoughtful questioning, this is the answer that emerged. Once the coat campaign was underway, the ultimate goal would be to measure the effectiveness of the coat collection and distribution effort over time to see if student tardiness and absences were impacted or whether any other positive outcomes were reported.

Educating Yourself About Business

If you've considered launching your own business (and hopefully sharing profits with charity) or starting a nonprofit, and this chapter has added fuel to that fire, you may be looking for more concrete resources to help you get started. There are experienced people who are willing to mentor you, excellent how-to books, online educational opportunities, and many free online resources you can download to begin the process. The following suggestions offer some ways to arm yourself with the knowledge, skills, experience, and tools needed to start a business such as a social venture. While you may not be able to utilize all of them, several of these resources are free and widely available and might give you the boost you need to turn your ideas into reality.

Connect with a Mentor or Advisor

Oprah Winfrey said, "A mentor is someone who allows you to see the hope inside yourself." A mentor can be any peer or adult with experience and expertise in your specific area of interest. A mentor is someone with whom you build a relationship over time, who shares wisdom earned through lived experience and guides you along your journey. Mentors provide business knowledge and professional advice. They offer connections to other people who can help you develop your idea. If you're able to identify someone in your community who has started a business or runs a nonprofit you admire, reach out to them

and ask if you can spend some time together. Even if it is difficult to find a mentor in your community, try to find an adult in the business or nonprofit world whose work you admire and inquire if they would be an advisor on your project. An advisor is someone who would provide advice on a specific project, sharing their expertise, reviewing plans, and asking questions to help you be successful. It may seem intimidating to reach out to a stranger and ask for their help, but professionals are typically honored to receive these calls and happy to help.

Take Advantage of Free Resources Online

- The US Small Business Administration offers a free online course for young entrepreneurs that's about 30 minutes long. It introduces the basics of creating and financing a successful business and provides simple step-by-step instructions on how to evaluate your ideas, choose the best financing options, and legally register your business.

- Biz Kid$ (bizkids.com) is a financial literacy initiative that teaches young people about money and business. While some of its features are geared toward younger kids, it provides basic resources for young entrepreneurs, like simple marketing and sales tips, sample business plans, and profiles of other young entrepreneurs.

- A company called Palo Alto Software offers Bplans (bplans.com), a website filled with free business-planning templates and resources.

- Young Founders Club (youngfoundersinstitute.com/young-founders-club) is a national network of entrepreneurship clubs led by middle and high school students. Students build or grow their start-up companies, learn about entrepreneurship, and have the opportunity to compete for funding. Young Founders Clubs work directly with the Young Founders Institute, a collaboration with colleges like Duke, the Massachusetts Institute of Technology, and the University of North Carolina at Chapel Hill. The Young Founders Institute hopes to shape the next generation of innovators.

Find Step-by-Step Instructions and Templates in the Following Books:

- *Social Entrepreneurship: From Issue to Viable Plan* by Terri D. Barreiro and Melissa M. Stone (This book is a little more advanced but has tons of good information.)

- *Social Entrepreneurship: What Everyone Needs to Know* by David Bornstein and Susan Davis

- *10 Steps to Your First Small Business (For Teens)* by Adam Lean

- *The Social Entrepreneur's Playbook: Pressure Test, Plan, Launch and Scale Your Enterprise* by Ian C. MacMillan and James D. Thompson (Much like *Social Entrepreneurship*, this one is excellent but geared toward college students and adults.)

- *Teen Entrepreneur Toolbox: The Small Business Guide for Teens* by Anthony ONeal

- *Crushing It! How Great Entrepreneurs Build Their Business and Influence—and How You Can, Too* by Gary Vaynerchuk

---

STARTUP SQUAD

The Startup Squad (thestartupsquad.com) is a brand and book series that believes entrepreneurship can empower girls to develop important life skills, follow their passions, and reach their potential. While the books series is written for younger readers and the organization generally focuses on younger girls, the website features inspiring stories of "Girl CEOs," an informative blog, and free downloadable tips and tools that teen entrepreneurs will find helpful. The Startup Squad also amplifies great charitable organizations that you might want to learn about. Its social media (@startupsquad) features "Teen Topic" live events and highlights inspiring female founders.

Get Inspired

Perhaps the best way to envision yourself creating a social enterprise is to read or hear about the ways other young people have done it. You need to "see it to be it." Next are three examples of teen social entrepreneurs who have successfully launched businesses or created nonprofit organizations that are making an impact on important issues. Of course, there are countless innovators and pioneers from whom we can learn so much, and there may even be young leaders in your own community who have had similar success. If you want to read more stories that might inspire you, take a look at the list of books written by and about social entrepreneurs at the end of this chapter.

Mikaila Ulmer, Me & the Bees Lemonade

Mikaila Ulmer launched her company, Me & the Bees Lemonade (meandthebees.com), when she was only four years old. Her parents encouraged her to come up with an idea to enter a local children's business competition, and she used her fascination with bees and her love of her great-grandmother's flaxseed lemonade recipe to create a lemonade sweetened with honey. From the beginning, Mikaila has donated a portion of profits from sales of her lemonade to local and international organizations dedicated to saving honeybees. Her motto is "Buy a Bottle, Save a Bee." Mikaila, now a teenager, also touts the health benefits of the flaxseed found in her lemonade, which is sold at supermarkets, food trucks, and restaurants.

Haile Thomas and HAPPY

When her father developed type 2 diabetes, eight-year-old Haile Thomas was determined to help her father's dietary habits in order to improve his health. As Haile educated herself on plant-based diets and integrative nutrition, she found her passion. At the age of 10, after her family had reversed her father's diabetes, she founded a nonprofit called HAPPY (thehappyorg.org), which stands for Healthy, Active, Positive, Purposeful Youth. HAPPY provides peer-to-peer learning experiences to empower "at-risk" and underserved elementary and middle school students. The organization teaches kids its "3 Keys to HAPPY": nurturing physical health, mental health, and soul development. HAPPY's programs include plant-based nutrition and culinary summer camps, school visits and tours, and a virtual academy.

The Students of the Rise Collection

In 2019, a group of teens from the South Side of Chicago joined a 16-week entrepreneurship program at the Black Ecosystem (blackecosystem.org), a community organization devoted to empowering underserved kids and teens through entrepreneurship training and self-improvement programs. The teens behind the Rise Collection put their artwork on products like T-shirts and hoodies and sell them online. Their goal is to work together to help stop violence through entrepreneurship and economic empowerment. Each design is personal to the designer, and every purchase supports kids and teens in Chicago.

USING TECH TO MAKE AN IMPACT

Here are a few more inspiring examples of teen entrepreneurs who are using technology to make a difference in the lives of others:

◇ Science enthusiast Erin Smith **LEARNED** that people with Parkinson's Disease all share a similar facial expression that makes them look distant. She built a diagnostic system called FacePrint that can detect changes in facial expressions and may allow doctors to diagnose conditions like Parkinson's much sooner.

◇ When programmer Sanil Chawla was a sophomore in high school, he wanted to start a web development company but quickly realized that there were many barriers for teens who try to start businesses. He did some **RESEARCH** and discovered fiscal sponsorship. This involves a nonprofit extending its own legal status and support to smaller organizations with a similar mission. He developed software to automate the required paperwork and founded Hack+, a nonprofit that provides free fiscal sponsorship to student-led charitable organizations. Hack+ partners with major companies like Google, Microsoft, and Amazon to help these student organizations handle the legal and organizational hurdles so they can focus on their mission of doing good.

◇ Langston Whitlock met a veteran who was experiencing homelessness at a community outreach event. The veteran mentioned that he was having difficulty finding rides to medical appointments. A woman name Ja'Nese Jean asked if Langston could build an app to meet that need. She and Langston co-founded SAFETRIP, a ride-sharing app geared toward people living marginally or experiencing homelessness and the elderly. The app allows patients, caretakers, and healthcare providers to book medical transportation, and SAFETRIP accepts insurance. SAFETRIP is another example of a teen keeping eyes, ears, and heart open; **NOTICING** a need; and using skills and talent to fill it.

The Tools You Need:
Training, Grants, and Mentorship

There are many established organizations that believe in the power of youth leadership and innovation, and they offer their considerable resources—intellectual and financial—to help teens succeed. The organizations described below, as well as other nonprofits and some corporations with strong philanthropic missions, provide funding, educational resources, and mentorship opportunities for teen entrepreneurs. If you have a solid plan for a social venture or even an unpolished idea with potential, you should explore these programs and apply for funding. You need to do the work and be thoughtful and thorough in the application process, but the opportunity to receive resources and mentorship that can help you make a difference in the world is worth the time and effort. It's easy to doubt yourself or think that others won't share your vision, but you'll never know what you might have achieved if you don't apply. As hockey legend Wayne Gretzky famously said, "You miss 100 percent of the shots you don't take."

Ashoka is all about cultivating changemakers and is best known to have blazed the trail on youth social entrepreneurship with the launch of Youth Venture (ashoka.org/youth-venture) in 1996. The vision of Youth Venture is to create a society where every young person has the confidence, ability, and support to be a changemaker for the good of all. If this sounds like a lofty goal, that's because it is. Youth Venture encourages teens to take action and solve the problems they encounter around them by launching and leading their own social ventures with the intention of leaving a positive mark on their school, college, home, and career. Ashoka does this work by engaging influencers in a young person's community—educators, parents, companies, nonprofit organizations, and government leaders—to support them in their journey. Ashoka offers many tools and resources, including mentorship, support networks, connection through storytelling, and financial services.

DECA (deca.org) is an organization that prepares emerging leaders and entrepreneurs in marketing, finance, hospitality, and management in high schools and colleges. DECA is based in chapters within schools (if your school doesn't have a chapter, you can start one). Each chapter must have a minimum of 10 members and an advisor, and dues are typically less than $10 per person per year. DECA members compete in competitions and challenges, like an innovation challenge, a digital presentation skills challenge, and a social media marketing challenge. DECA also offers educational conferences, an emerging leader series, and scholarships (sponsored by corporate partners). DECA is a robust program that can help you build a network, serve your community, gain experience, and develop skills, all while meeting and working with peers with similar interests.

The Diamond Challenge (diamondchallenge.org) is a global high school entrepreneurial challenge for teams of two to four students created in 2012 by University of Delaware Horn Entrepreneurship. Since it's based at a university, it's backed by educational methodologies and offers a unique opportunity for teens to learn about entrepreneurship while putting their ideas into action. The competition offers an impressive $100,000 in prizes and resources to help students take their ideas to the next level.

DoSomething.org (dosomething.org) is the largest nonprofit devoted exclusively to young people and social change, engaging with millions of teens across the United States and in over 130 countries around the world. DoSomething.org members join campaigns focused on volunteer work, social change, and civic action to make an impact on causes they care about. The organization also offers what it calls "easy" scholarship money. You are not required to submit essays, your grade point average, recommendations, or applications. You enter to win by doing community service, and you can apply for more than one scholarship at a time. DoSomething.org has really tapped into youth activism and leadership in a way that gets teens excited and allows them to use their strengths as digital natives, encouraging them to use social media to spread the word about volunteer opportunities and campaigns they've created (see more about using social media for good in chapter 7). It's a terrific model and probably the best example I've seen of harnessing the energy and passion of young people and empowering them with the tools to make a difference.

The Heartwarming Project, sponsored by the Hershey Company (the hersheycompany.com), offers $250 action grants to teens who create projects to jump-start inclusion, empathy, and kindness in their school or community.

The Jacobson Institute Innovator Competition (jacobsoninstitute
.org/innovator-competition) encourages an entrepreneurial mindset
in teens, allowing high school students to pitch an idea for a business or product twice per year, in fall and spring. Financial support
(up to $3,000) is provided, along with feedback from successful
entrepreneurs.

Peace First (peacefirst.org) is a nonprofit organization dedicated to
helping young people around the world become powerful peace-
makers. For over 20 years, Peace First has successfully worked with
young people in all 50 US states and in 82 countries, investing in their
ideas, providing them with tools and skills, and connecting them
with like-minded kids around the world. Through the Peace First
Challenge, the organization inspires young people to identify a social
justice issue that they care about and develop a strategy to solve it
using the tools of compassion, courage, and collaborative leadership.
The Peace First Challenge is open to young people ages 13–25 anywhere in the world. By accepting the challenge, participants receive
tools, resources, digital mentors, and access to mini grants up to $250.

Riley's Way (rileysway.org) is a grassroots organization devoted to
inspiring teen leadership, promoting connection between young
people, and supporting social entrepreneurship. The Riley's Way
Foundation is named for a nine-year-old girl who tragically passed
away on the last night of summer camp in 2014. Her family launched
the foundation in her memory to empower young leaders to use
kindness and empathy to create meaningful connections and positive change. Riley's Way believes that kind leaders will build a better
world. To that end, it runs several programs, including a three-year
kindness curriculum for elementary schools and a partnership
council between public and private school students, both in New
York City. Its national programs include an annual Youth Leadership
Retreat and the Call for Kindness, an annual grant application process
that allows teens to submit proposals to receive funding for projects
that inspire kindness, support the community, and bring people
together. Grant recipients then participate in the organization's Kind
Leadership Series.

The W.I.S.E. Award from the National Museum of Education
(nmoe.org/student-ideas-better-americatm) is an ongoing contest

with no deadlines. To enter, suggest a new way to teach or demonstrate an educational concept (such as a scientific concept), an idea for a new product, or an improvement to an existing product or procedure. Prize money is awarded monthly, and winners can apply to be inducted into the National Gallery for America's Young Inventors.

KITCHEN TABLE KINDNESS TIP: GET CRAFTY, GET BAKING, AND EARN MONEY FOR CHARITY

If you are crafty and **CREATIVE**, you can use your talents to make and sell unique items and donate a portion of proceeds to charity. You might make beaded bracelets or other jewelry, knit hats, upcycle and paint gently used jean jackets, or personalize white sneakers with custom designs. The sky is the limit on what you can create, and if you share your goal of donating a portion of proceeds to charity, customers may be even more inclined to make a purchase. You can sell your items at a craft fair or farmers' market or set up an online shop on Etsy, Shopify, or Amazon Handmade.

If your talents lie in the kitchen and you'd like to sell cookies, candy, jelly, or other food items, be sure to do your **RESEARCH** around the cottage laws in your state. Cottage food laws govern the production and sale of processed foods by individuals. If you are producing the food at home, there may be rules around having your kitchen inspected. In some states, you may be able to sell your items at a roadside stand or a farmers' market, and while you can promote your products online, selling food on the internet or shipping it across state lines is often restricted.

Expand Your Knowledge

You may already be a fan of the products and services of some successful social ventures. Any time you purchase a product from a company that then donates some portion of its proceeds to charity, you are supporting a social enterprise and, hopefully, becoming more aware of the cause it champions. Just a few popular examples are Ethos water, KIND bars, TOMS shoes, and FEED bags. While these are huge, successful companies, they all began with the vision of a passionate person who cared about helping others. Several great books have been written about these folks and others like them. Reading these stories may inspire you to think about social entrepreneurship and the ways in which your talents and passion might be used to create a business or a community program that does good for others. Some of these books even offer advice and instructions for starting your own social venture.

1. *The Promise of a Pencil: How an Ordinary Person Can Create Extraordinary Change* by Adam Braun, founder of Pencils of Promise

2. *Mo's Bows: A Young Person's Guide to Start-Up Success* by Moziah Bridges with Tramica Morris

3. *Girls Who Run the World: 31 CEOs Who Mean Business* by Diana Kapp

4. *Do the KIND Thing: Think Boundlessly, Work Purposefully, Live Passionately* by Daniel Lubetzky, founder and CEO of KIND

5. *Start Something That Matters* by Blake Mycoskie, chief shoe giver at TOMS

6. *You Got This! Unleash Your Awesomeness, Find Your Path, and Change Your World* by Maya S. Penn

7. *Bee Fearless: Dream Like A Kid* by Mikaila Ulmer

8. *Dream First, Details Later: How to Quit Overthinking & Make It Happen!* by Ellen Marie Bennett

9. *Steve Jobs: Thinking Differently* by Patricia Lakin

10. *The Responsible Company: What We've Learned from Patagonia's First 40 Years* by Yvon Chouinard and Vincent Stanley

NOW IT'S YOUR TURN

Jot down some notes about the ideas that have been sparked by this chapter. How might you explore social entrepreneurship?

Ask yourself:

◇ What's the one issue I care most about?

◇ Go through "The 5 Whys" in this chapter to help you get to the heart of the actual problem and some possible solutions.

- Who is suffering?

- What is the problem or issue that causes the suffering?

- What is a possible solution to the problem?

◇ How might a social enterprise solve the problem?

- Who would benefit?

- What are the costs of and barriers to launching this venture?

◇ Who can I ask to help me brainstorm and get this idea off the ground? Who might be my mentor?

◇ Use the space below to write down any business or product ideas you have and how you might incorporate charitable giving into your business plan.

Turn Time *Off* into Time *On*

Exploring Internships, Community Service Projects, and Youth Leadership

During winter, spring, and summer vacation, you finally have time away from your classes and school-related extracurricular activities. When you get these breaks, you may want to relax and unplug from academic pressures and responsibilities. And taking care of yourself and giving yourself permission to *do nothing* (if you can) is important and well deserved. Of course, you may have other demands, like working a part-time job, training for sports, or studying for standardized tests. But if you find yourself with some free time after getting a little much-needed rest, take the opportunity to explore ways to give back to your community. There are many local and national organizations that would welcome your talents, energy, and effort during your time off from school. You'll gain valuable experience as you connect with others in your community and learn about the important work being done by nonprofits. And you'll feel great about the way you've chosen to turn time *off* into time *on*—for the good of others.

In this chapter, you'll **LEARN** about a variety of different school-break service opportunities around the country and be encouraged to create projects in your own community. You'll find starting points for **RESEARCHING** scholarships, funding opportunities, and internships, as well as suggestions for ways to **CREATIVELY SHARE** your ideas to support your applications for these grants and spots in selective programs. I also encourage you to **NOTICE** the needs of others around you and across the globe and to **MAKE TIME TO VOLUNTEER**.

Creating Service Opportunities Close to Home

Throughout this chapter, you'll see the names of established programs and organizations that would likely welcome your involvement when you're on a school break. However, while working with national nonprofits like Habitat for Humanity or traveling to volunteer in a national park are wonderful, life-enriching experiences, there is also so much you can do to help the people and organizations in your own community during your school breaks. I've included some recommendations for ways to get involved locally, and I hope you'll keep your eyes, ears, and heart open for these opportunities and others like them.

Summer Break (Two to Three Months)

Schools in the United States are typically closed during the summer months, in some areas for as long as three months. It's a great time to explore setting up a regular volunteer opportunity in your community or create service projects for yourself and your friends. Often, service hours earned in the summer are applicable toward school service requirements, and even if you don't have required hours for school, volunteering keeps you busy and provides meaningful experiences and life skills. These experiences may come in handy while writing college essays or interviewing for a job, and they will certainly make you feel good about the way you spent your summer vacation. Below are just a few ideas to get you started, but any of the suggestions found throughout this book can be applied to the months of free time that the summer can provide.

- Commit to a weekly (or even daily!) **VOLUNTEER** shift at a non-profit you already support during the school year. During summer break, deepen your commitment to the organization and ask to take on additional tasks and responsibilities.

- Gather a group of friends to host a series of **FUNDRAISING** activities in support of a specific charity. The laid-back summer months are a great time for a variety of easy, fun, and crowd-pleasing fund-raisers that will attract atten-tion and encourage friends and other teens to volunteer. Organize a car wash, lemon-ade stand, bake sale, drive-in movie night, swim-a-thon, or another of the projects described in chapter 4.

- Become a regular **VOLUNTEER** at a local park, community garden, farmers' market, community-supported agri-culture (CSA) farm, or green space. These areas are particu-larly active during the summer months, and they may need additional help to replace volunteers who depart on vacation. If formal volunteering isn't possible, gather a group of friends to clean and beautify a local green space every month.

- If you are interested in politics and social justice, volunteer in the campaign office of a local candidate who is seeking office in an upcoming election. These offices typically need help answering phones, making calls, stuffing envelopes, managing social media accounts, and running errands. Find a candidate whose policies, ideas, and values align with your own, and reach out to offer your **TIME** and **CREATIVE** talents.

- **VOLUNTEER** as a counselor at a local camp or summer program for younger kids. You might also find a family in your neighborhood who needs child care during the long school break but can't afford to pay a babysitter. Becoming a friend and mentor to a younger child is a fun and meaningful way to spend your time during the summer months, and your time can be a huge help to working parents in your community.

Winter and Spring Breaks (One to Two Weeks)

Depending on where you go to school and what type of school you attend, you may have anywhere from a few days to two weeks off during the December holiday season and again in the late winter or spring. These shorter breaks can be a good time to relax and unplug, catch up on schoolwork, visit with family, or work additional hours at a part-time job. You might also use this time to continue or deepen volunteer work you do during the school year. At a minimum, you should consider the ways that a few free days can be spent helping others as well as making time for yourself.

- Offer to rake leaves, mow the lawn, shovel snow, or spread salt on icy sidewalks for ill or elderly neighbors.

- In the warmer months, once the ground has thawed, gather a group of friends to do a park cleanup and plant bulbs so that flowers will bloom in the summer.

- Winter and spring are great times for you and your family to sort through closets, toy boxes, and bookshelves to find items that you and your siblings have outgrown or no longer use and **DONATE** these to children and families in need in your community. Remember that anything you donate should be very gently used, clean, free of holes and tears, and in good shape. Never donate anything in such a condition that you wouldn't wear or use the item yourself. As you collect clothing or shoes to donate from your closet, consider whether you would feel comfortable giving them to a friend. If not, they might not be good enough to donate.

Ensuring that the items you are donating are of high quality shows respect to the recipients and allows them to maintain their dignity. Donating gently used items is also a great way to encourage reusing, recycling, and upcycling and reduces the amount of waste clogging our landfills (making this a particularly great activity for April, which is considered Earth Month).

- Use a short break to **RESEARCH** and contact a nonprofit you'd like to support, and see if you can schedule your orientation and training during this time. These orientations are typically done during the day, so taking care of it when you are not in school will set you up to begin volunteering when you find time in your normal schedule.

Community Service and Youth Leadership Programs

The following organizations are well-established national nonprofits that provide service and leadership opportunities around the country (and sometimes around the world) through affiliates, chapters, and clubs.

- **generationOn** (generationon.org), which is the youth division of Points of Light (pointsoflight.org), inspires, equips, and mobilizes millions of people to take action to change the world. generationOn Clubs provide comprehensive resources for kids and teens ages 5–18 to start and sustain service clubs in schools and community organizations. It also sponsors campaigns throughout the year (including an annual Family Volunteer Day the weekend before Thanksgiving in partnership with Disney) to engage youth and families in service. These campaigns are widely promoted, and provide project ideas, lesson plans, and grant opportunities to support volunteerism. generationOn also offers training for educators and lots of free resources for schools engaging in service learning. If your school is not connected to generationOn, you can **RESEARCH** the resources it offers and suggest them to school administrators. Whether you're on your own, with your family, or on a school break, generationOn offers many ways for you to begin to get involved in your community. It's free and easy to join to gain access to these resources, and members are encouraged to use a tool on the website to upload project ideas, share stories, and track their impact.

- **Habitat for Humanity** (habitat.org) was founded in 1976 with a mission to help families build and improve places to call home. Over the course of its history, Habitat has helped more than 35 million people by providing them with affordable and safe homes. Today, the organization works in all 50 US states and in over 70 countries worldwide. Teens can get involved building houses over school breaks in a variety of ways: through student-initiated high school chapters that work in local communities; through the Collegiate Challenge (see the Habitat for Humanity Collegiate Challenge sidebar); and through a special weeklong event called Act! Speak! Build! Week, which helps young people educate themselves, advocate for policy changes, and move community members to social action.

THE HABITAT FOR HUMANITY COLLEGIATE CHALLENGE

For over 30 years, the Habitat for Humanity Collegiate Challenge has offered alternative school break opportunities for students throughout the United States. The program is offered year-round. Teens who want to participate need to recruit five or more friends ages 16 or older. Volunteers select a location either close to home or somewhere across the country that they are interested in traveling to. Collegiate Challenge volunteers learn about substandard living conditions and how affordable housing builds strength, stability, and self-reliance for homeowners, meaning you'll see not just a house being built or repaired but the people behind it. It's a great way to **LEARN** to understand big issues—such as poverty and homelessness— while having a real and lasting impact on the lives of individual people affected.

- The **Red Cross** is an international relief organization with a long and storied history. Originally established in Geneva in 1863 as the International Committee for Relief to the Wounded, the American Red Cross (redcross.org) was founded by Clara Barton in 1881. The Red Cross is a relief organization that helps people in the United States and around the world with emergency assistance, disaster relief, and emergency preparedness education. There are many ways to volunteer with the Red Cross, and it engages teens through its school-based clubs and National Youth Council.

- **Youth Service America** (ysa.org), founded in 1986, supports a culture of young people committed to giving back in meaningful ways throughout their lifetimes. YSA offers a number of great programs that could be a good fit for your school break schedule: Global Youth Service Day (the largest youth service and civic action event in the world, and the only one that celebrates all youth, ages 5–25—typically celebrated at the end of April) and Semester of Service; grant funding for service programs; online training and resources through the YSA Knowledge Center; and recognition through awards, profiles of young volunteers, and visibility campaigns.

Service Near and Far

If you have the resources, ability, and opportunity to leave your hometown, there are a few ways that you can combine service with travel. The following programs offer diverse and meaningful ways to volunteer and learn about different issues while traveling (or in your own area, if you happen to live near one of these organizations). Be sure to do your homework so you understand the best ways to support the communities you will be visiting.

- **Youth Rebuilding New Orleans** (yrno.com) is a grassroots organization that engages young Louisiana residents and other groups of young people in helping to rebuild distressed and foreclosed homes in New Orleans, Louisiana. The refurbished homes are sold to teachers to stabilize neighborhoods. Minors who wish to participate (under age 18) must have a signed waiver, and teens under the age of 15 must be accompanied by an adult while volunteering.

- If you are an animal lover or have an interest in farming and agriculture, you might enjoy spending your school break volunteering on a local farm in your state or at one of the two locations of **Farm Sanctuary** (farmsanctuary.org), which are in upstate New York and near Los Angeles, California. Farm Sanctuary is a nonprofit working to promote compassionate vegan living and protect farm animals from cruelty. The Farm Sanctuary website offers programs and educational resources for anyone interested in veganism and farm-animal rescue.

- The **Best Friends Animal Sanctuary** (bestfriends.org) in Kanab, Utah, is another option for animal lovers who live in the region or are able to travel there. It is the largest no-kill pet sanctuary in the United States, and family and youth volunteers are welcome. If you can't make it to Kanab but would like to work with animals in another state, the Best Friends Animal Society website provides links to regional programs in Salt Lake City, Utah; Los Angeles, California; New York City, New York; and Atlanta, Georgia. The website also hosts a searchable database of other animal-rescue organizations and shelters across the United States that might welcome youth volunteers.

- **Give Kids the World Village** (gktw.org) is an 89-acre nonprofit resort in Kissimmee, Florida, that provides free weeklong vacations and access to Walt Disney World for children with life-threatening illnesses and their families. You can sign up for three- or four-hour volunteer shifts any day of the week. The long list of volunteer activities includes scooping ice cream, staffing rides like the carousel, participating in evening entertainment, and wearing costumes to bring beloved characters to life.

- If you're lucky enough to live near or be able to travel to one of America's national parks, they provide perfect educational and volunteer opportunities for teens who care about the environment and preserving our natural resources—or teens who simply enjoy the outdoors! Volunteers of all ages are welcome at most national parks. You can search for appropriate opportunities through the **National Park Service's volunteer program** (nps.gov /getinvolved/volunteer.htm).

Internships

My oldest daughter (now a young adult) has had a passion for service her whole life, and she hopes to work in the nonprofit sector once she finishes her education. During her teen years, she actively sought internships at nonprofit organizations. She worked for an organization that provides essential goods and educational resources to families with babies born into poverty. She also worked in fundraising and marketing for the Michael J. Fox Foundation, which supports research in Parkinson's disease, a condition that has touched our own family. She was a social media intern at an organization that helps underresourced teens prepare for and apply to college.

My daughter was fortunate to have lots of different options because we live in a city with many social service and nonprofit organizations. She also hustled and was tenacious about finding these opportunities. She educated herself on the organizations she was targeting and was relentless in emailing and following up. Most of her experiences were unpaid, and we were fortunate that she was able to work in those roles without needing to earn a salary—a luxury that many teens can't afford. There are internships that provide salary or a stipend, and you should always ask about this when inquiring. If you are able to do internship work at a nonprofit, with or without being paid, you will certainly gain great experience, skills, and knowledge that you can use when applying to college, technical school, or future full-time employment—and for lifelong giving back.

As you begin your online search for an internship in the nonprofit sector, it's important to start close to home. If you or your family have a relationship with a local organization—for example, if you've donated to or volunteered there in the past—you should reach out to the administrators to ask about internships. Your school may also be a good source for networking, as many schools that offer service-learning curriculum or have service requirements collaborate with local nonprofits. Even if you have no connection at all but are familiar with an organization that does important work in your community, you can always reach out to the executive director or the director of volunteers by sending a "cold" email introduction or making a call to inquire.

Author and entrepreneur Tam Pham gives some simple, down-to-earth advice in his book, *How to Land Your Dream Internship*:

1. Figure out what you want to do, who you want to help, and what you have to offer. You can do all of this by doing some online **RESEARCH** and setting up informational interviews with organizations doing good work in areas you care about. Make note of the following:

    ◇ You are not asking for a job in an informational interview. Rather, you are just having a conversation and learning more about the organization, making a connection, and expressing your interest.

    ◇ You can get an informational interview by networking (asking people you know if they can connect you to someone in the organization) or by cold emailing.

2. Pham recommends putting together a simple résumé that lists your relevant classes, experience, and areas of interest. This need not be fancy or lengthy. It should just highlight your skills and talents and any applicable work you've done or courses you've taken. If you send out your résumé in an email, you should include a brief cover letter in the body of your email explaining why you are reaching out.

3. Do your **RESEARCH** before contacting the nonprofit. You should understand and support the mission of the organization. If you can, take a look at its financials and sources of funding. You should understand how it operates and the ways that your unique skills and talents might benefit its operation. Inquiring about an internship is just like applying for a job. You want to put your best foot forward. You want to be articulate and confident and show that you've done your homework about the organization. Take notes and be familiar with facts and figures (How many people does the organization help each year? How many pounds of food are distributed? How does the organization change lives?). In this way, you should try to be overprepared for the interview: able to respond to any question, **SHARE YOUR KNOWLEDGE**, and offer ways that you are uniquely qualified to be a part of the team.

4. **EXPRESS GRATITUDE**! No matter what happens, be sure to reach out afterward to thank everyone who helped you or spoke to you throughout the process.

5. Perhaps the best tip of all: Believe in yourself, and remember that you have something to contribute. You have skills, energy, and talents, but most importantly, you care about the problem that the organization works to solve. You want to help—and that's worth a great deal.

KITCHEN TABLE KINDNESS TIP: VIRTUAL INTERNSHIPS

During the COVID-19 pandemic, employment, volunteering, and education often took place virtually, and this change sparked a widespread conversation about the need or desire to gather in offices. Internships also moved online, and in some instances, this shift to virtual work opened up opportunities for teens and young adults who might not have otherwise been considered for positions because of geography or ability. This improved accessibility is one of the silver linings of the pandemic, and one that will likely continue long after offices and schools have reopened fully. In terms of kitchen table kindness, you now have the ability to apply for virtual internships that allow you to fundraise, connect with isolated and elderly people via FaceTime or Zoom, manage social media accounts for nonprofits, engage in political activism by writing to elected officials or starting petitions, and participate in a variety of other opportunities that are described throughout this book. This chapter includes some databases where you will find available internships, many of which are virtual. You can also search for "virtual internships" in your area.

As you begin searching for an internship, you can make use of several national organizations that can help you connect with nonprofits:

- AmeriCorps (americorps.gov) *Note: Most AmeriCorps opportunities are for people over the age of 18, but some applications are open to teens who are 16–17 years old.*

- Chegg Internships (internships.com)

- Find Your Summer (findyoursummer.org) *For Jewish teens.*

- InternshipFinder (internshipfinder.com)
- National Council of Nonprofits (councilofnonprofits.org)
- Teens in Public Service (teensinpublicservice.org)
- VolunteerMatch (volunteermatch.org)

NOW IT'S YOUR TURN

Jot down some notes about the ideas that have been sparked by this chapter. So, how will you turn time *off* into time *on*?
Ask yourself:

◦ What time will I have available to give back? What are my responsibilities during school breaks? Do I need to earn money, study for standardized tests, take additional classes, finish college applications, help care for family members?

◦ What activities do I enjoy or prefer, and what am I good at? How can I translate those skills into a service project or internship? For example: Do I enjoy the outdoors and working with my hands, or do I prefer sitting at a desk in an office? Am I good with kids or seniors? Do I thrive as part of a group, or am I better working solo?

◦ Is traveling to another state or out of the country a possibility for me? If so, where could I go, and what kind of volunteer work would I like to do there?

#BeKind

Harnessing the Positive Power
of Social Media

In the same way that a cold or virus can be transmitted from one person to another, emotions—both positive and negative—can also be passed between people. This phenomenon of "emotional contagion" has been scientifically proven, and I bet you've seen this play out in your own life. When you are with anxious people, you're likely to feel more nervous. When you are with someone who is angry and fired up, you may start to feel agitated as well. But the opposite is also true. When you are in the presence of someone who is calm and kind, your heart rate slows, and you feel more peaceful. When you surround yourself with people who are generally happy and positive, you naturally feel more optimistic yourself.

Social media is a virtual universe of emotions, opinions, and ideas that circulate widely very quickly. This isn't always a good thing, but it can be. A 2013 study of emotional contagion focused on social media, specifically the Facebook News Feed posts of nearly 700,000 people, to investigate our emotional responses to certain types of posts. The researchers considered a post to be "positive" or "negative" if it had at least one positive or negative word in it. They adjusted the number of positive or negative posts people would see in their News Feeds. When people were exposed to fewer positive posts, the scientists found that people then produced fewer positive posts and more negative posts. When people were exposed to fewer negative posts, the opposite happened, and the tone of their posts became more positive. The experiment demonstrates that the emotions expressed by others on social media influence our own emotions—and the emotions of millions of other social media users.

Perhaps what is most striking about all of this is that these results were found by studying online habits only. No face-to-face interaction between the participants was included in the study. It may be hard to believe that a person's positive or negative mood can be relayed only through words and emojis on a screen, or the lack of them, but I think we've all experienced this to be true at some point. The power of a poorly worded text and the perceived meaning behind an emoji cannot be changed once they are out in the universe.

The specific social platform being used is unimportant, and it would be impossible to mention all of them given how frequently new apps rise in popularity and use. The important point is that you understand and appreciate the incredible power you possess in your ability to use (or abuse) social media. Of course, I encourage you to use your powers for *good*, to spread positive, helpful, encouraging, hopeful, and kind messages that can ultimately have a big impact on people, organizations, and society.

Throughout the chapter, you'll see ways to use the internet and social media to **RESEARCH AND LEARN** about important social justice issues and to connect with organizations that are making an impact on them. A wide world of ideas and possibilities is literally at your fingertips. I hope you'll also be inspired to use social media to **RAISE AWARENESS**, to **SHARE YOUR CREATIVITY** and express your point of view, and to amplify the messages of individuals and organizations that are spreading positive messages.

Amplify the Good

There are so many ways you can engage with social media to create and amplify kindness and to spark positive change. I probably don't need to mention those ways here, as you are experts in this area and are innovating and adapting to a changing technological landscape all the time. But the internet and social media are powerful tools for you as a changemaker and future leader, so it's important to use this power for good.

Social media can be a wonderful tool when it's used to share messages of hope, kindness, acceptance, tolerance, inclusion, and love. Images, words, music, and videos can combine to create a very powerful emotional response in a person who is scrolling through. I've had this experience myself, and I often want to amplify the messages that truly move me so that my followers can share the experience.

Conversely, the ability of social media to harm others—through shaming and humiliation—is powerful as well, and I hope you'll do everything you can to minimize the spread of such messages, both by never participating in harmful behavior on social media yourself and by intervening when you see lies, cyberbullying, or hateful messages. It may sound obvious, but you can virtually stand up for a person or group of people who are being harmed by messages that you see on social media. Keep your eyes open and **NOTICE** when a vulnerable person or group is being maligned online. You have the power to intercede, to blast positive messages that can silence the perpetrator and drown out the mean, hurtful things that are often posted and circulated. Remember that you have two choices when you see people abusing social media by using it to spread cruelty and hate: you can be part of the problem by sharing negativity or remaining silent, or you can be part of the solution by modeling good behavior and commenting words of support and encouragement.

CHANNELING KINDNESS WITH THE BORN THIS WAY FOUNDATION

The award-winning singer-songwriter and actress Lady Gaga (whose real name is Stefani Germanotta) talks openly about her struggles with mental illness. She was bullied from a young age and remembers being thrown in a trash can at school as classmates looked on. She also openly shares that she was sexually assaulted at the age of 19. She struggled with anxiety and depression in adolescence and throughout college. She was able to receive professional help for her illness and went on to achieve success and fame as a performer. Lady Gaga and her mother, Cynthia Germanotta, cofounded the Born This Way Foundation in 2012 to support the mental health of young people and work with them to create a kinder and braver world. Through programming, youth-led conversation, and strategic partnerships, their mission is to make kindness cool, to validate the emotions of young people, and to eliminate the stigma surrounding mental health.

Born This Way Foundation recognized the absence of positive stories in the media, and in 2017–2018, it recruited over 100 young people ages 15–24 from across the United States to identify and broadcast acts of kindness they saw in their everyday lives and communities. Their stories are published on the Channel Kindness website (channelkindness.org), are spread across the program's social media channels, and have now been published in a book, *Channel Kindness: Stories of Kindness and Community*. Of particular interest in terms of social media are the many campaigns and challenges Born this Way Foundation promotes through its platforms, including #MultiplyingGood in honor of World Kindness Day and #BeKind21, an annual initiative that inspires teens to take a pledge to do one act of kindness each day from September 1 to September 21. #BeKind21 is based on the theory that it takes 21 days to form a habit. Born This Way Foundation uses the significant and growing power of social media to destigmatize mental illness and to amplify positivity, bravery, and kindness.

In addition to being a platform for spreading kindness, social media also offers a means of shining a light on injustice and sparking change. You can promote civic engagement by sharing your own passions on social media and encouraging others to do the same. You can repost messages that are important for people to hear; spread the word about marches, petitions, and walk-outs; and support political activism in your community, elsewhere in the country, or around the world. As we witnessed during Black Lives Matter protests in 2020 and beyond, social media is how movements grow to include hundreds, thousands, or millions of people in a very short period of time. This is the breathtaking power of the internet and social media: it connects millions of people all over the world.

KITCHEN TABLE KINDNESS TIP: THE APRIL 29TH EXPERIMENT

Amy Krouse Rosenthal was an award-winning children's book author, memoirist, artist, and creator. She wrote 30 children's books—some of which you may remember from your own childhood or recognize from bookstore shelves, like *Yes Day!*, *I Wish You More*, *Little Pea*, and *Exclamation Mark*. She passed away from cancer, and her family started the Amy Krouse Rosenthal Foundation (amykrouserosenthalfoundation.org) to honor her memory by funding ovarian cancer research and childhood literacy initiatives. The foundation also honors Rosenthal's legacy by continuing some of her many creative projects, including the April 29th Experiment. April 29 was Amy's birthday, and she asked that every year on 4/29, at exactly 4:29 p.m., everyone in the world text the words *I love you* to someone. That's all she wanted for her birthday. Amy believed in the power of the collective. Here's one tiny thing you can do from your own kitchen table, and something really good that you can promote to all of your social networks: set an alarm for April 29 every year at 4:29 p.m. to remind yourself to text "I love you" to someone that you love. Imagine if *everyone* did this? It's such a small thing, and yet it could spread love around the globe. It could (maybe) even change the world.

Start Scrolling and Sharing the Good

Below are some established, verified social media accounts that focus on spreading positive, empowering messages. Of course, this list doesn't include every positive account—there are far too many organizations and people sharing kindness online to list in one book, and new accounts pop up regularly, so it would be hard to keep an up-to-the-minute list. These are just some of the accounts that might interest you, and they might point you in the direction of similar accounts through their interactions with other nonprofits or influencers. This is the rabbit hole of social media, and it's helpful in finding the accounts you will want to follow and the messages you will amplify.

Remember that you get to decide which messages to support and amplify. As a savvy social media user, you will likely come across hundreds of accounts that are promoting positive messages around social justice issues that you care about. Be sure to properly vet the ones you support, which means thoroughly **RESEARCHING** them, both on their websites and on their social media pages, to make sure you believe in their mission and philosophy and agree with their tactics and messages. Since there are so many, I've broken them down by category.

Clean Water / The Environment

- Charity: Water (charitywater.org; @charitywater)
- Fridays for Future (fridaysforfuture.org; @fridaysforfuture)
- Greta Thunberg (@gretathunberg)
- WaterAid (wateraid.org; @wateraid)
- Water.org (water.org; @water)

Economic Injustice / Poverty

- CARE (care.org; @careorg)
- Global Citizen (globalcitizen.org; @glblctzn)
- Red Nose Day (rednoseday.org; @rednosedayusa)
- Save the Children (savethechildren.org; @savethechildren)
- UNICEF (unicef.org; @unicef)

Health

- Bill & Melinda Gates Foundation (gatesfoundation.org; @gatesfoundation)
- (RED) (red.org; @red)

Hunger

- #HashtagLunchbag (hashtaglunchbag.org; @hashtaglunchbag)
- No Kid Hungry (nokidhungry.org; @nokidhungry)

Kindness

- Dare to Be Kind Movement (daretobekindmovement.global; @daretobekindmovement)
- Good Deeds Day (good-deeds-day.org; @gooddeedsday)
- Kindness.org (kindness.org; @kindnessorg)
- The Kindness Rocks Project (thekindnessrocksproject.com; @thekindnessrocksproject)
- PIFOR (Pay It Forward) (pifor.net; @pifor_net)
- Random Acts of Kindness (randomactsofkindness.org; @rakfoundation)
- Tank's Goods News (tanksgoodnews.com; @tanksgoodnews)
- Upworthy (upworthy.com; @upworthy)

Political Activism

- Rock the Vote (rockthevote.org; @rockthevote)
- Students Demand Action (studentsdemandaction.org; @studentsdemand)
- Teens Resist (teensresist.com; @teensresist)
- We Vote Next (wevotenext.us; @eighteenx18)

Racial Inequality

- Black Lives Matter (blacklivesmatter.com; @blklivesmatter)
- Color of Change (colorofchange.org; @colorofchange)
- NAACP (naacp.org; @naacp)

Refugees

- Choose Love (us.choose.love; @chooselove)

Women and Girls

- Girls Rising (girlrising.org; @girlrising)
- Girl Up (girlup.org; @girlupcampaign)
- Me Too (metoomvmt.org; @metoomvmt)
- Play Like a Girl (iplaylikeagirl.org; @iplaylikeagirl)
- She Should Run (sheshouldrun.org; @sheshouldrun)
- TIME'S UP Now (timesupnow.org; @timesupnow)

MAKING CONNECTIONS BY TEACHING TECH

If you've ever tried to text, share a video, or FaceTime with a grand-parent or elderly relative, you likely know that smartphone technology can be baffling for older folks who weren't raised with it. The buttons are small, the screens are confusing, and everything seems to move and change quickly. Instead of feeling frustrated with their lack of ability, why not reach out and help them (or other older adults in your community)? Your practiced skill in using technology is one of your many strengths, and your willingness to share this skill is a great service to older people hoping to stay connected to loved ones and the world around them through social media and other technology. Teaching tech will allow you to show off an area where you shine and help you gain perspective and patience in dealing with folks who need a little extra time and help. Intergenerational volunteering, which means volunteering with people from a vastly different age group than your own, benefits everyone involved. While you are teaching an older family member, friend, or neighbor how to set up and use online accounts, they are teaching you about life, telling you a funny story, complimenting your skills, or giving you advice. Your local public library or senior service agency might provide opportunities to connect with elderly neighbors to provide this type of support. You'll both gain so much, and the exchange will make you feel great.

NOW IT'S YOUR TURN

Jot down some notes about the ideas that have been sparked by this chapter. So, how can you use social media to spread positive messages, kindness, and hope?

Ask yourself:

◇ What are my favorite ways to access social media?

◇ What are the most positive social media accounts I follow, and how can I amplify their messages?

◇ What are my favorite charities and causes, and do they have social media accounts? If so, how can I support them?

◇ How could I intervene in online bullying?

8

Not-So-Random Acts of Kindness

52 Intentional Ways to Spread Kindness Every Day

"Kindness is free. Sprinkle that stuff everywhere."
—*Unknown*

The quote above is one of my favorites, and it is so true. Kindness costs you *nothing*, and spreading it around generously is certainly better than doing the opposite! If you approach other people with a positive attitude, they'll likely reflect it back to you. And your actions create a ripple effect, like a stone dropped into water. One simple act of kindness from you might change the whole trajectory of another person's day (or even life). I don't really love the expression "random acts of kindness," because I think you need to be *intentional* about your actions. You need to keep your eyes, ears, heart, and mind open to **NOTICE** the ways that you can spread love, kindness, and acceptance in the world, every day, as you walk through your very busy and distracted life. It's a subtle shift in your mindset and the way you approach the world. If you give it a try, I promise it will change your life for the better. It just feels good to live with purpose, to be known as a kind person, and to make others feel seen and appreciated.

Read on for 52 *not-so-random* acts of kindness (one for each week of the year) that you can try out. Of course, these are only 52 of the limitless ways you can be kind and generous. Your list should be as big as your heart and as vast as your imagination. This is the ultimate **PAY-IT-FORWARD** moment. I hope you'll use the list below as your launching pad.

1. Smile at a stranger.

2. Hold the door for the person behind you.

3. **EXPRESS GRATITUDE** to the crossing guard, doorman, or person at the front desk—every time.

4. **THANK** a person using their name (if you know it or can see it on an ID badge).

5. Leave a sticky note with an encouraging word on a classmate's locker or desk.

6. Say "Have a good day" to a least one person every day, *and mean it.*

7. Take out the trash for a neighbor.

8. Throw out your own trash, and don't litter.

9. Pick up litter that you **NOTICE** another person drop, and throw it away.

10. Carry something heavy for someone you **NOTICE** is struggling.

11. Help a visually impaired or disabled person safely cross the street. Say hello, and ask first!

12. Give a genuine compliment to a stranger or a friend.

13. Carry change or some granola bars to give away in case you encounter a person who is experiencing hunger or homelessness.

14. If you can, **PAY IT FORWARD** by paying for the person behind you in line at the coffee shop or the drive-through lane.

15. Take the time to **SHARE** your expertise and teach someone a new skill.

16. Say **THANK YOU,** a lot. It's been said that you should say please and thank you at least 50 times per day. Saying "you're welcome!" is a kind thing too!

17. Prepare a meal for your family.

18. On a snowy or icy day, shovel the walkway for a neighbor or clear the snow from their car.

19. Pick up groceries for a neighbor who is ill or homebound.

20. Give high fives to little kids or smile and wave if they are across the way.

21. **SHARE YOUR KNOWLEDGE AND TALENTS** by teaching an elderly person to text (or email, FaceTime, Zoom, or use other apps and technology that might help them stay connected to loved ones).

22. **LEARN** a few helpful, friendly phrases in a foreign language that is spoken in your community (this can include American Sign Language).

23. Respectfully acknowledge holidays that are special to your friends, whether or not they are in your faith tradition.

24. Give appropriate holiday greetings to a person of another faith.

25. If you're able, when you get change in the coffee shop, put a few coins or dollar bills in the tip jar for the staff.

26. Write a note of **THANKS** to the server on your restaurant check (in addition to tipping).

27. Bring a cup of hot chocolate to the school crossing guard or maintenance worker on a cold or rainy day (or a cold bottle of water on a hot day).

28. Send a handwritten **THANK-YOU** note when you get a gift. If you can't make that happen, at least send a thoughtfully worded email or text or call the gift giver on the phone in a timely fashion.

29. If you shop on Amazon, enroll in AmazonSmile (and make sure to shop at the AmazonSmile web address!) so you **RAISE MONEY** for a

charity of your choice when a portion of the money you spend is donated to it each time you shop.

30. Mark the birthdays of friends and relatives in your calendar and make sure to acknowledge those special days—even if it's just with a short text or quick phone call.

31. At the end of the school year, be sure to **THANK** your teachers. If you can, write them a note. They'll appreciate it more than you know.

32. Be sure to **THANK** everyone who helps you and keeps you safe and healthy at school—security, maintenance, office staff, cafeteria workers, nurses, etc.

33. Call out bullying and unkind behavior when you see it, and stand up for kids who are having a tough time.

34. Forgive someone who has frustrated you. Take the high road.

35. Include people. Exclusion is a form of bullying.

36. **DONATE** things you've outgrown (clothes, books, sports equipment, toys) to someone who needs them.

37. Let someone go ahead of you in line.

38. Help around your house without being asked.

39. Be an active listener when someone else is talking.

40. Warmly welcome new people (into your school, apartment building, club, team, or workplace).

41. Check in on a friend who you **NOTICE** is having a hard time.

42. **MAKE TIME TO VOLUNTEER** to read aloud to little kids.

43. Share what you have with others.

44. Always stop and support a lemonade stand.

45. Admit when you are wrong, and make an honest and sincere apology.

46. Leave a **THANK-YOU** note for the garbage collector or delivery person.

47. Be gentle with people. Be a peacemaker.

48. If you borrow something from someone, return it promptly and in good condition. If it's a piece of clothing or a bag, leave a small **THANK-YOU** note in a pocket for the person to find later.

49. **SHARE YOUR KNOWLEDGE AND TALENTS** by offering to help a classmate who is struggling in a subject you understand.

50. Return your shopping cart.

51. Call or text someone who care about you, just to check in.

52. Be kind, even when no one is watching, even when your kindness might not be repaid.

KITCHEN TABLE KINDNESS TIP:
NOT-SO-RANDOM ACTS OF KINDNESS AT HOME

I love to tell the story about the time my son woke up before dawn on the day his older sister was leaving on an early flight for her first year of college. He covered the front door with bright yellow sticky notes that said things like, "You're going to do great!" and "I'm going to miss you." Imagine being nervous about the next chapter of your life and finding a display like that as you are about to walk out the door. I believe in the loving power of the sticky note (pro tip: keep a stack in your bag or locker so you are always prepared to leave a kind note for someone). There is so much you can do at home to help others. You can **EXPRESS GRATITUDE**, love, and support to members of your own family. You can **NOTICE** when a neighbor seems ill or sad and write them a note and slip it under their door. You can bake cookies, package them up individually, and take them to school to pass out to anyone who looks like they can use a smile. In your free time, while you're hanging out, watching a movie, or relaxing on the weekend, you can make paper flowers or Valentines for isolated elderly people and then find a time to deliver them. If you are **CREATIVE** and artsy, be sure to keep colorful construction paper and markers handy so that, if you're feeling inspired and have the time, you can create some things that you will "randomly" share with others when you are out in the world. This chapter, and this whole book, is about being intentional, mindful, and open to living your life with kindness, compassion and gratitude—and there's nothing random about that.

NOW IT'S YOUR TURN

Create your own bucket list of not-so-random acts of kindness. If you can't think of things you might do in the future, try to recall some of the kind and generous things you've done or witnessed others doing in recent months, and write those down to inspire you.

Create a kindness challenge for yourself with a different act of kindness for each day of the month.

Recommended Resources

There are many excellent organizations and websites promoting youth volunteerism and offering tips, resources, and inspiring stories, as well as databases of volunteer opportunities that can be searched by zip code. I've listed many of these organizations throughout the text of *Simple Acts,* but I've also included them here for quick reference. Most of these organizations also use social media to spread the good word about service and kindness, so be sure to follow accounts that are of interest, and notice when other similar sites are "suggested for you." I hope the following list provides you with a good start as you embark on a lifetime of kindness and service.

National Organizations and Useful Websites

- All Hands and Hearts (allhandsandhearts.org)
- AmeriCorps (americorps.gov)
- Big Brothers Big Sisters of America (bbbs.org)
- Charter for Compassion (charterforcompassion.org)
- Create the Good (createthegood.org)
- Doing Good Together (doinggoodtogether.org)
- DoSomething.org (dosomething.org)
- Family-to-Family (family-to-family.org)
- generationON (generationon.org)
- The Great Kindness Challenge (thegreatkindnesschallenge.com)
- Idealist (idealist.org)
- The Joy Team (thejoyteam.org)
- JustServe (justserve.org)

- KindnessEvolution (kindnessevolution.org)
- Kindness Matters 365 (kindnessmatters365.org)
- Kindness.org (kindness.org)
- Learning to Give (learningtogive.org)
- ME to WE (metowe.com)
- The Nature Conservancy (nature.org)
- Pennies of Time (penniesoftime.com)
- Points of Light (pointsoflight.org)
  - ◇ The Points of Light Global Network includes partner organizations like United Way, HandsOn, and many others. You can search for your local affiliate at pointsoflight.org/global-network.
- Project Sunshine (projectsunshine.org)
- Ronald McDonald House Charities (rmhc.org)
- SpreadKindness.org (spreadkindness.org)
- Strength Behind Stars (strengthbehindstars.org)
- Thankful (thankful.org)
- United Way (unitedway.org)
- VolunTEEN Nation (volunteennation.org)
- VolunteerMatch (volunteermatch.org)
- Volunteers of America (voa.org)
- World Kindness Movement (theworldkindnessmovement.org)

Bibliography

Ain, Stewart. "The Logic of 'Mandatory Volunteerism.'" *New York Times*, March 23, 2003. nytimes.com/2003/03/23/nyregion/the-logic-of-mandatory-volunteerism.html

Andersen, Susan M., and Nancy Murphy. "Mandatory Community Service: Citizenship Education or Involuntary Servitude?" *Service Learning, General*, Paper 107, November 1999. digitalcommons.unomaha.edu/slceslgen/107.

Annie E. Casey Foundation. "Children in Poverty by Age Group in the United States." Kids Count Data Center, last updated September 2020. datacenter.kidscount.org/data/tables/5650-children-in-poverty-by-age-group.

Barreiro, Terri D., and Melissa M. Stone. *Social Entrepreneurship: From Issue to Viable Plan*. New York: Business Expert Press, 2013.

Carlson, Michelle C., Kirk I. Erickson, Arthur F. Kramer, Michelle W. Voss, Natalie Bolea, Michelle Mielke, Sylvia McGill, George W. Rebok, Teresa Seeman, and Linda P. Fried. "Evidence for Neurocognitive Plasticity in At-Risk Older Adults: The Experience Corps Program." *The Journals of Gerontology: Series A* 64A, no. 12 (December 2009): 1275–1282. doi.org/10.1093/gerona/glp117.

Chokshi, Niraj. "94 Percent of U.S. Teachers Spend Their Own Money on School Supplies, Survey Finds." *New York Times*, May 16, 2018. nytimes.com/2018/05/16/us/teachers-school-supplies.html.

Corporation for National and Community Service. "Educating for Active Citizenship: Service-Learning, School-Based Service, and Civic Engagement." *Youth Helping America* 2 (March 2006). files.eric.ed.gov/fulltext/ED494175.pdf.

————. "The Health Benefits of Volunteering: A Review of Recent Research." Office of Research and Policy Development, April 2007. americorps.gov/sites/default/files/evidenceexchange/FR_2007 _TheHealthBenefitsofVolunteering_1.pdf.

DoSomething.org. "The DoSomething.Org Index on Young People and Volunteering: 2012: The Year of Friends with Benefits." Accessed via USA Swimming on April 8, 2021. usaswimming .org/docs/default-source/clubsdocuments/volunteers/athletes -as-volunteers/index-on-young-people-and-volunteering-the -year-of-friends-with-benefits.pdf.

Emmons, R. A., and M. E. McCullough. "Counting Blessings Versus Burdens: An Experimental Investigation of Gratitude and Subjective Well-Being in Daily Life." *Journal of Personality and Social Psychology* 84, no. 2 (2003): 377–389. greatergood.berkeley.edu/pdfs/Gratitude PDFs/6Emmons-Blessings Burdens.pdf.

Entrepreneur. "Meet 16 Teen Founders Who Are Building Big Businesses—and Making Big Money." August 20, 2019. entrepreneur.com/slideshow/337852.

Feeding America. "Facts About Child Hunger." Accessed July 1, 2021. feedingamerica.org/hunger-in-america/child-hunger-facts.

————. *The Impact of the Coronavirus on Food Insecurity in 2020 & 2021.* March 2021. feedingamerica.org/sites/default/files/2021-03 /National%20Projections%20Brief_3.9.2021_0.pdf.

Kramer, Adam D. I., Jamie E. Guillory, and Jeffrey T. Hancock. "Experimental Evidence of Massive-Scale Emotional Contagion in Social Media Networks." *Proceedings of the National Academy of Sciences of the United States of America* 111, no. 24 (June 17, 2014): 8788–8790. doi.org/10.1073/pnas.1320040111.

Kumar, A., and N. Epley. "Undervaluing Gratitude: Expressers Misunderstood the Consequences of Showing Appreciation." *Psychological Science* 29, no. 9 (2018): 1423–1435. doi.org/10.1177 /0956797618772506.

MacMillan, Ian C., and James D. Thompson. *The Social Entrepreneur's Playbook: Pressure Test, Plan, Launch and Scale Your Enterprise,* expanded ed. Philadelphia: Wharton School Press, 2013.

National Diaper Bank Network. "What Is Diaper Need?" Accessed June 1, 2020. nationaldiaperbanknetwork.org/diaper-need.

Oosterhoff, Benjamin. "Volunteer or Voluntold: Does Required Service Benefit Youth?" *Psychology Today*, January 7, 2019. psychologytoday.com/sg/blog/civically-engaged/201901/volunteer-or-voluntold-does-required-service-benefit-youth.

Pham, Tam. *How to Land Your Dream Internship: Proven Step-by-Step System to Gain Real World Experience.* Self-published: CreateSpace, 2016.

Piliavin, Jane Allyn, and Erica Siegl. "Health Benefits of Volunteering in the Wisconsin Longitudinal Study." *Journal of Health and Social Behavior* 48, no. 4 (December 1, 2007): 450–464. doi.org/10.1177/002214650704800408.

Samuelson, Chidike. "How Generation Z Is Altering the Face of Entrepreneurship for Good." *Entrepreneur*, November 24, 2020. entrepreneur.com/article/358930.

Schroeder, Bernard. "A Majority of Gen Z Aspires to Be Entrepreneurs and Perhaps Delay or Skip College. Why That Might Be a Good Idea." *Forbes*, February 18, 2020. forbes.com/sites/bernhardschroeder/2020/02/18/a-majority-of-gen-z-aspires-to-be-entrepreneurs-and-perhaps-delay-or-skip-college-why-that-might-be-a-good-idea.

Smolla, Rodney A. "The Constitutionality of Mandatory Public School Community Service Programs." *Law and Contemporary Problems* 62, no. 4, (Autumn 1999), 113–139. doi.org/10.2307/1192269.

US Department of Agriculture Economic Research Service. "Food Security in the U.S." Last updated February 24, 2021. ers.usda.gov/topics/food-nutrition-assistance/food-security-in-the-us.

US Department of Housing and Urban Development Public Affairs. "HUD Releases 2020 Annual Homeless Assessment Report 1: Homelessness Increasing Even Prior to Pandemic." News release no. 21-041, March 18, 2021. hud.gov/press/press_releases_media_advisories/hud_no_21_041.

Varner, Joyce. "The Elder Orphans: Who Are They?" *The Alabama Nurse* 32, no. 3 (September–November 2005): 19–20.

World Bank. "Poverty Overview." Last updated October 7, 2020. worldbank.org/en/topic/poverty/overview.

Index

About the Author

Natalie Silverstein, MPH, is an author, speaker, consultant, and passionate advocate for family and youth service. Her first book, *Simple Acts: The Busy Family's Guide to Giving Back,* was published by Gryphon House in 2019 and was named one of the "10 Books for Parents Who Want to Raise Kind Kids" by *HuffPost.*

In September 2013, Natalie launched the first local affiliate of Doing Good Together (doinggoodtogether.org), a Minneapolis-based nonprofit with the mission of helping parents raise kids who care and contribute. As the New York area coordinator, she curates a free monthly email listing of family-friendly service opportunities that is distributed to thousands of subscribers. Natalie is a frequent writer and speaker on the importance of service and acts of kindness in family life, and she has presented to parents, educators, and children across the country. She has appeared on many popular podcasts and on the *3rd Hour of TODAY* on NBC. Her personal essays have appeared on parenting websites Grown and Flown, Red Tricycle, and Mommy Poppins, and on the Moms Don't Have Time to Write platform on Medium.

Natalie earned an undergraduate degree in health policy and administration from Providence College and a master's degree in public health from Yale. She lives in New York City with her husband and three children.

Other Great Resources from Free Spirit

Going Blue
A Teen Guide to Saving
Our Oceans, Lakes,
Rivers, & Wetlands
*by Cathryn Berger Kaye, M.A.,
and Philippe Cousteau with
EarthEcho International*
For ages 11 & up.
*160 pp.; PB; full-color;
6" x 9".*

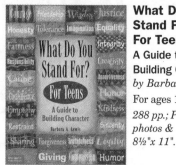

**What Do You
Stand For?
For Teens**
A Guide to
Building Character
by Barbara A. Lewis
For ages 11 & up.
*288 pp.; PB; B&W
photos & illust.;
8½"x 11".*

**The Teen Guide to
Global Action**
How to Connect with
Others (Near & Far) to
Create Social Change
by Barbara A. Lewis
For ages 12 & up.
*144 pp.; PB; 2-color;
illust.; 7" x 9".*

**Real Kids, Real Stories,
Real Change**
Courageous Actions Around
the World
by Garth Sundem
For ages 9–13.
176 pp.; PB; 2-color; 5¼" x 7½".
*Free Leader's Guide
freespirit.com / leader*

**What Do You
Really Want?**
How to Set a Goal and Go
for It! A Guide for Teens
(Revised &
Updated Edition)
by Beverly K. Bachel
For ages 11 & up.
*160 pp.; PB; 2- color;
6" x 9".*

**Real Kids, Real Stories,
Real Character**
Choices That Matter Around
the World
by Garth Sundem
For ages 9–13.
168 pp.; PB; 2-color; 5¼"x 7½".
*Free Leader's Guide
freespirit.com / leader*

Interested in purchasing multiple quantities and receiving volume discounts?
Contact edsales@freespirit.com or call 1.800.735.7323 and ask for Education Sales.

Many Free Spirit authors are available for speaking engagements, workshops, and keynotes.
Contact speakers@freespirit.com or call 1.800.735.7323.

For pricing information, to place an order, or to request a free catalog, contact:

Free Spirit Publishing
An Imprint of Teacher Created Materials
**6325 Sandburg Road, Suite 100
Minneapolis, MN 55427-3674**

**toll-free 800.735.7323 • local 612.338.2068
fax 612.337.5050 • help4kids@freespirit.com • freespirit.com**